Paths to College and Career
English Language Arts

Research, Decision Making, and Forming Positions

Published by Jossey-Bass
A Wiley Brand
One Montgomery Street, Suite 1000, San Francisco, CA 94104-4594—www.josseybass.com

Jossey-Bass books and products are available through most bookstores. To contact Jossey-Bass directly call our Customer Care Department within the U.S. at 800-956-7739, outside the U.S. at 317-572-3986, or fax 317-572-4002.

Wiley publishes in a variety of print and electronic formats and by print-on-demand. Some material included with standard print versions of this book may not be included in e-books or in print-on-demand. If this book refers to media such as a CD or DVD that is not included in the version you purchased, you may download this material at http://booksupport.wiley.com. For more information about Wiley products, visit www.wiley.com.

ISBN: 978-1-119-10527-5

Printed in the United States of America

FIRST EDITION
PB Printing   10 9 8 7 6 5 4

CONTENTS

Unit 2   67

Unit 3 143

Rachel Carson's Quote

"In nature nothing exists alone."

—Rachel Carson, writer, scientist, and ecologist

Learning from Frightful's Perspective

Chapter 1

Name: _____

Date: _____

Chapter 1: "Frightful Takes Off" **Words I Found Difficult:** jesses (9) culvert (11) tierce (19) **Glossary:** talons—*noun:* the claw of the bird perch—*noun:* anything upon which a bird rests prey—*noun:* an animal hunted or killed for food by another animal predator—*noun:* an animal that hunts other animals for food	**Focus question:** Identify one human relationship or one animal relationship that Frightful has in this chapter. Do you think this relationship is helpful or harmful to Frightful's survival? Explain your thoughts.	
	My thoughts:	**Evidence from the text:**

Learning from Frightful's Perspective
Chapter 2

Name: _____

Date: _____

Chapter 2: "Frightful Goes to Falcon School"	Focus question: What is something that Frightful learns from her relationship with Chup?
Words I Found Difficult:	
Glossary:	
aerie—*noun:* the nest of a bird on a cliff, mountaintop, or high place	
eyases—*noun:* undeveloped birds, not feathered or ready for flight, nestlings	**My thoughts:** / **Evidence from the text:**

Chapter 2, "Frightful Goes to Falcon School"

Peregrine Falcon Facts

Name: _____

Date: _____

Directions:

1. Each member of your group should choose a different topic from the four listed next.
2. Then, read the text pages in the parentheses that correspond to your topic.
3. As you read the text, find at least three facts, or evidence, that support the topic.
4. Record what you've learned about peregrine falcons in the space provided.
5. Also refer to your homework, Learning from Frightful's Perspective: Chapter 2, to get additional information.

Physical description of adults and eyases (pages 21, 22, 29)

_____

_____

_____

Habitat (pages 21 and 22)

_____

_____

_____

Mating (page 22)

_____

_____

_____

Hunting and eating (pages 23, 24, 27, 28)

_____

_____

_____

_____

Welcome Back

By Susan Nagle-Schwartz

Full speed ahead! The peregrine falcon perched high on a cliff ledge spots a starling below. His keen vision allows him to focus on the target. Head pointed down, wings and feet tucked in, he beings his dive.

A peregrine's dive or "stoop" can reach speeds of up to 200 miles an hour. No speeding ticket for this guy, though. Instead, success! He strikes the starling, circles back and grabs it with his sharp talons. Mission accomplished.

Just as he's catching his next meal, a fellow falcon streaks by at a level cruising speed of 55 miles per hour. Sunlight reflects off of his blue-gray back, a black moustache lines the sides of his face beneath a black head and white cheeks. Long pointed wings permit him to easily shift position while in flight.

The peregrine falcon is a magnificent bird and we are fortunate to be able to enjoy these agile flyers today. Once one of the most widespread birds of prey, the peregrine almost completely disappeared from our skies.

In the 1950s and 1960s, farmers used DDT, *dichloro-diphenyl-trichloroethane,* to kill insects that damaged their crops. Birds that the peregrine falcon fed on were eating the insects with DDT in them, which built up in the falcon's body, causing the female falcons to lay thin-shelled eggs. When they sat on their eggs to keep them warm, the eggs broke before the chicks could hatch.

Hoping to help the falcons, scientists began raising chicks in captivity. Eggs were hatched in laboratories under the scientists' watchful eyes. Hand puppets that looked like the mother falcons were used to feed the babies. That way, they remained wild because they thought "mom" was feeding them. In 1974, the first peregrine falcons raised in captivity were released into the wild.

Raising falcons in captivity, as well as other actions taken during the 1970s, helped to increase their numbers. The use of DDT was banned in 1972, and the following year the peregrine falcon became protected under the Endangered Species Act. Due to all of these efforts, these remarkable birds have made a comeback from 235 known nesting pairs in 1975, to an estimated 2,000 pairs in the United States and Canada today.

Thanks to the actions of scientists and others who cared enough to save the peregrine falcon, we are able to, once again, enjoy these aerial acrobats.

—*Susan Nagle-Schwartz is a freelance writer interested in wildlife conservation, in Pennsylvania.*

Reprinted from *Skipping Stones*, March–April 2010. Used by permission.

EXPEDITIONARY
LEARNING

Learning from Frightful's Perspective

Chapter 3

Name: _____

Date: _____

Chapter 3: "The Eyases Get on Wing" **Words I Found Difficult:** **Glossary:** nictitating membrane—*noun:* a thin membrane found in many animals at the inner angle or beneath the lower lid of the eye and capable of extending across the eyeball fledgling—*noun:* a young bird	**Focus question:** What are some of the physical and behavioral changes that occur as Drum, Lady, and Duchess become young peregrine falcons? Use evidence from the text to support your thoughts.	
	My thoughts:	**Evidence from the text:**

EXPEDITIONARY
LEARNING

Frightful's Relationships

Excerpts from Chapter 3

Name: _____

Date: _____

"Frightful ate the rabbit while the eyases watched, twisting their heads from side to side and calling 'pseee' when she swallowed." (p. 32)

What relationship of Frightful's does this excerpt refer to?

Why is this relationship important?

- -

"Then he learned that she didn't like groundhogs. She had tried one and abandoned it to him. She also didn't like skunks or rats." (p. 35)

What relationship of Frightful's does this excerpt refer to?

Why is this relationship important?

- -

"Frightful saw the food fall onto the blazing-star leaves and seedpods, then flew to a tall hemlock at the top of the cliff. Sitting among the lacy needles, the image of the one mountain among thousands, the one tree among millions." (p. 39)

What relationship of Frightful's does this excerpt refer to?

Why is this relationship important?

- -

"Chup answered from above. He dove, scattered a flock of ducks, and brought one back to the aerie. He dropped it without slowing down, then flew over the cliff." (p. 42)

What relationship of Frightful's does this excerpt refer to?

Why is this relationship important?

- -

© Copyright Public Consulting Group, Inc. Created for Public Consulting Group, Inc. by Expeditionary Learning with a perpetual license granted to Expeditionary Learning Outward Bound, Inc.

Notice and Wonder Graphic Organizer

Name: _____

Date: _____

Notice	Wonder

Tracing an Argument Graphic Organizer

Name: _____

Date: _____

SL.6.3: I can outline a speaker's argument and specific claims.

I can determine whether a speaker's argument is supported by reasons and evidence or not.

Title of the Article or Video:	Author or Speaker:

Author's Claim:	Evidence to Support the Claim:
	Is the claim supported by sufficient evidence? Yes No
Author's Claim:	**Evidence to Support the Claim:**
	Is the claim supported by sufficient evidence? Yes No
Author's Claim:	**Evidence to Support the Claim:**
	Is the claim supported by sufficient evidence? Yes No

After identifying the claims and evidence presented by this author, what argument do you think she or he is making?

After evaluating the evidence that supports each claim, is the overall argument supported by sufficient evidence? Explain why or why not.

Learning from Frightful's Perspective
Chapter 4

Name: _____

Date: _____

Chapter 4: "The Wilderness Tests the Eyases" **Words I Found Difficult:** **Glossary:** instinct—*noun:* a natural ability or inclination juvenile—*adjective:* showing incomplete development; immature, childish pilgrimage—*noun:* a journey	**Focus question:** Peregrine falcons use their instincts to know when they should migrate south. What "signs in nature" signal the falcon that it is time to migrate? Use evidence from the text to support your thoughts. Include the page number(s) where you found your evidence.	
	My thoughts:	**Evidence from the text:**

"The Exterminator"

By Kirsten Weir

Can an old pesticide that is banned in most countries defeat one of the world's worst diseases?

Few Americans ever give much thought to malaria. That wasn't always so. Malaria once infected—and killed—many people in the United States. During the Civil War, more than a million soldiers fell ill with the disease.

By the middle of the 20th century, malaria had been wiped out in the United States, Canada and northern Europe. But it continues to be a serious health problem in many tropical countries. Malaria kills an estimated 2 million people every year, most of them children under age 5. Despite an international effort to control the disease, malaria rates in Africa have risen over the past few years. "It's going in the wrong direction," said Roger Bate, the director of Africa Fighting Malaria, a nonprofit research and advocacy group.

Bate is one of several health officials now pushing for broader use of DDT (dichloro-diphenyl-trichloroethane), a chemical that played an important role in kicking malaria out of the United States. They argue that DDT is the best option available for saving lives. But DDT is a touchy subject because it has been banned in the United States and many other countries for decades.

Bad Air

People once believed that breathing nasty swamp air caused malaria. In fact, the word malaria is Italian for "bad air."

Toward the end of the 19th century, scientists identified the true cause: a single-celled parasite they named Plasmodium. About the same time, scientists also discovered that mosquitoes act as vectors for the parasite, passing it on when they bite people. A vector is an organism that spreads disease-causing agents from host to host without harm to itself.

The malaria parasites need warm temperatures to develop inside mosquitoes, and the balmy southeastern United States was once hit hard by the disease. Malaria existed nearly everywhere mosquitoes did. During steamy summers, the disease reached as far north as Montreal. Changes in living habits—a shift toward city living, better sanitation, and the use of window screens—were largely responsible for the eradication of malaria, but DDT also played a part. DDT is an *insecticide,* a chemical that kills insects. In the 1930s and 1940s, when the U.S. government made a serious effort to wipe out malaria, DDT was one of its preferred weapons. It was sprayed on swamps and other wet areas where mosquitoes bred. Small amounts were also applied to some household walls in rural communities.

By 1951, malaria was gone from the United States, but DDT was still used for other purposes. Huge quantities of it were sprayed by airplane on farmland to kill the insect pests that feasted on cotton and other crops. At first, no one worried about the possible effects of the chemical on the environment. Then, in 1962, an ecologist named Rachel Carson captured the country's attention with her book *Silent Spring*, which detailed the dangers of DDT.

Carson described the damage done by DTT, which persisted in nature for years without breaking down. The chemical first built up in the tissues of fish. It then accumulated inside eagles and other birds of prey that ate the fish. It caused the birds' eggshells to become thin and brittle. The eggs cracked under their own weight, sending bird populations into a nosedive. The U.S. government responded by banning DDT in 1972.

Seriously Sick

Malaria begins with flulike symptoms: fever, sweating, chills, headaches, muscle aches, and nausea. The symptoms come and go every 48–72 hours. Without treatment, the disease can get much worse. The parasites infect and destroy red blood cells, which can lead to severe anemia, a condition in which the concentration of red blood cells is too low to supply enough oxygen to the body's tissues. Infected blood cells can also clump together and stick to the body's blood vessels, blocking blood flow to the brain. The result is often blindness, brain damage, or death.

Drugs are available to treat malaria, though many are expensive. To be most effective, the drugs must be taken before the disease becomes severe. Poor families in places such as rural Africa often cannot afford the drugs, or they put off going for treatment until it's too late.

Some prophylactic, or preventive, medications are also available. When given to uninfected people, they attack the parasite if it ever gets into the body. But the prophylactic drugs are expensive and hard on the body. Travelers can safely take them for a few weeks or months, but the pills are too toxic for people living in malaria-affected countries to tolerate for long periods of time.

Double Whammy

Many other countries followed suit, including a number of nations that relied on DDT for malaria control. A handful of malaria-ridden countries have continued to use DDT to control the disease. But even in those countries, DDT is no longer dumped in mass quantities onto the land. It is applied only to the inside walls of houses. Because malaria mosquitoes bite after dusk, protecting people inside their homes can be very effective. DDT packs a double whammy: It repels most mosquitoes and kills those that get too close. It is by far the cheapest insecticide available and lasts twice as long as the alternatives.

South Africa was one nation that continued to use DDT after the United States banned the chemical. By 1996, South Africa had fewer than 10,000 annual malaria deaths. That year, the country switched from DDT to other insecticides. The new insecticides were also widely used in farming, and the overexposed mosquitoes quickly became resistant to the chemicals. By 2000, the number of deaths from malaria had risen to more than 60,000. At that point, South Africa turned back to DDT. Within three years, malaria infections dropped nearly to 1996 levels. In other countries where DDT has been used, from Ecuador to Sri Lanka, it has had similar positive effects.

Today, only about 20 countries use DDT for malaria control, according to Roger Bate. Many more could benefit, he says.

Killer Genes

Scientists have tried for decades to develop a vaccine to prevent malaria, without success. Dozens of different species of mosquito carry the parasite inside them, infecting people with their blood-sucking bites. To complicate things further, four different Plasmodium parasites cause malaria in humans. Because so many different species of mosquito and parasite are involved, and because Plasmodium's life cycle is so complex, a vaccine has so far been impossible to produce.

Still, researchers haven't given up. Many are looking for solutions in modern biotechnology. In 2002, scientists sequenced the genomes of the most common malaria parasite, Plasmodium falciparum, and one of its most common carriers, the mosquito Anopheles gambiae. A genome is the total genetic information in an organism.

Theoretically, scientists could use that genetic knowledge to tinker with the genome of the mosquito to make its immune system kill the parasite. Or researchers could tweak the genome of the parasite itself to render it less infectious or less deadly. Such tasks would take years to accomplish, if they can be achieved at all. But the genomes offer one more target in the fight against malaria.

Public Fear

Why don't more countries use the powerful insecticide? "DDT probably has more opponents than any other insecticide because of its historic use," explained Bate. "But it's mistaking the point! All of the problems associated with it in the past are down to the mess that was made of it in farming."

Some wealthy countries worry about the double standard of supporting the use of a chemical abroad that they've banned at home. The memory of *Silent Spring* and dying bald eagles also lingers. Most of the money that tropical countries use to fight malaria comes from international donors. Many of those donors are reluctant to fund the use of a chemical that scares so many people.

"Why [DDT] can't be dealt with rationally, as you'd deal with any other insecticide, I don't know," Janet Hemingway, the director of the Liverpool School of Tropical medicine, told *The New York Times*. "People get upset about DDT and merrily go and recommend an insecticide that is much more toxic."

Bate and many of his colleagues argue that the public's fear of DDT is unfounded. Billions of Americans were exposed to high amounts of DDT when it was used in agriculture, Bate said, without any harm to human health. And many scientists agree that the small amounts needed for malaria protection would likely have no significant effect on the environment.

Meanwhile, malaria is not going away. Some scientists estimate that malaria has killed half of all the people who have ever lived. Today, the disease claims two lives every minute. The most severely affected countries are in Africa, where the disease takes the life of one in every 20 children.

Some scientists worry that the situation could become even worse. As global warming heats up the planet, mosquitoes are spreading into areas where they once could not survive. Hotter temperatures also allow the Plasmodium parasite to develop faster inside the mosquito, infecting more people in a short amount of time.

Most scientists now think that eradicating malaria is impossible, given the complicated life cycle of the parasite. But chipping away at the disease is possible, and DDT has proved itself to be a valuable tool.

"The big picture is bad, but there are examples out there of what works," Bate said. "We need every tool in the arsenal!"

From CURRENT SCIENCE, *November 5, 2004. Copyright © 2004 by The Weekly Reader Corporation. Used by permission and not subject to Creative Commons license.*

EXPEDITIONARY
LEARNING

Learning from Frightful's Perspective

Chapter 5

Name: _____

Date: _____

Chapter 5: "Frightful Peregrinates" **Words I Found Difficult:** **Glossary:** current—*noun:* air or water moving continuously in a certain direction migration—*noun:* movement from one place, region, or climate to another	**Focus question:** As the weather changes, many other changes occur in Frightful's environment. These changes and the need to survive pull her in two different directions. What two directions is Frightful pulled in? Which direction does Frightful choose? Use evidence from the text to support your thoughts.	
	My thoughts:	**Evidence from the text:**

EXPEDITIONARY
LEARNING

Tracing an Argument Graphic Organizer

Name: _____

Date: _____

RI.6.8: I can identify the argument and specific claims in a text.

I can evaluate the argument and specific claims for sufficient evidence.

Title of the Article or Video:	Author or Speaker:

Author's Claim:	Evidence to Support the Claim:
	Is the claim supported by sufficient evidence? Yes No

Author's Claim:	Evidence to Support the Claim:
	Is the claim supported by sufficient evidence? Yes No

Author's Claim:	Evidence to the Support Claim:
	Is the claim supported by sufficient evidence? Yes No

After identifying the claims and evidence presented by this author, what argument do you think she or he is making?

After evaluating the evidence that supports each claim, is the overall argument supported by sufficient evidence? Explain why or why not.

Exit Ticket

Argument, Claims, and Evidence

Name: _____

Date: _____

Directions: Define the following:

1. Author's argument:

_____

_____

_____

_____

2. Claim:

_____

_____

_____

_____

3. Evidence:

_____

_____

_____

_____

EXPEDITIONARY
LEARNING

Learning from Frightful's Perspective

Chapter 6

Name: _____

Date: _____

Chapter 6: "Frightful Finds the Enemy"	Focus question: Who is the enemy that Frightful encounters? Why do they want to capture Frightful? Use evidence from the text to explain your answer.	
Words I Found Difficult:		
Glossary: hemlock tree—*noun:* evergreen coniferous trees of the pine family		
preened—*verb:* to smooth or clean (feathers) with the beak or bill	**My thoughts:**	**Evidence from the text:**
offense—*noun:* a crime		

Sidebar Task Card

Name: _____

Date: _____

Argument: DDT is the best option available for saving lives from malaria.		
Claim	**Claim**	**Claim**
Evidence	**Evidence**	**Evidence**
Is the evidence sufficient?	Is the evidence sufficient?	Is the evidence sufficient?
Why or why not?	Why or why not?	Why or why not?

Sidebar "Seriously Sick" Glossary

Name: _____

Date: _____

symptoms	*n.* changes in the body or mind that indicate that a disease is present
parasites	*n.* animals or plants that live in or on other animals or plants and get food or protection from them
anemia	*n.* a condition in which a person has fewer red blood cells than normal and feels very weak and tired
effective	*adj.* producing a result that is wanted
prophylactic	*adj.* designed to prevent disease
preventive	*adj.* used to stop something bad from happening
uninfected	*adj.* not containing germs that cause disease
toxic	*adj.* containing poisonous substances; poisonous
tolerate	*v.* to experience (something harmful or unpleasant) without being harmed

Sidebar "Killer Genes" Glossary

Name: _____

Date: _____

genes	*n.* the instructions inside every cell of a plant or animal on what the plant or animal is, what it looks like, how it is to survive, and how it will interact with its surrounding environment
genomes	*n.* all of the genetic materials of an organism
genetic	*adj.* of, relating to, or involving genes
vaccine	*n.* a substance that is usually injected into a person or animal to protect against a particular disease
species	*n.* a group of animals or plants that are similar and can produce young animals or plants
Plasmodium	*n.* a parasite that causes malaria
life cycle	*n.* the series of stages through which a living thing passes from the beginning of its life until its death
biotechnology	*n.* the use of living cells, bacteria, etc. to make useful products (such as new kinds of medicine)
organism	*n.* an individual living thing
theoretically	*adv.* relating to what is possible or imagined rather than to what is known to be true or real
immune system	*n.* the system that protects your body from diseases and infections

Learning from Frightful's Perspective

Chapter 7

Name: _____

Date: _____

Chapter 7: "Disaster Leads to Survival"	**Focus question:** In this chapter, Frightful survives a near-death experience thanks to a person named Jon. However, many peregrine falcons have not survived and the birds have become an endangered species. What are two things that have caused the death of many peregrine falcons? Use evidence from the text to support your answer.	
Words I Found Difficult:		
Glossary:		
pesticides—*noun:* chemicals used for killing pests, especially insects and rodents	**My thoughts:**	**Evidence from the text:**
mews—*noun:* enclosures for trained hawks		
destiny—*noun:* something that is to happen or has happened to a particular person or thing; lot or fortune		

Tracing an Argument Graphic Organizer

Name: _____

Date: _____

RI.6.8: I can identify the argument and specific claims in a text.

I can evaluate the argument and specific claims for sufficient evidence.

Title of the Article or Video:	Author or Speaker:

Author's Claim:	Evidence to Support the Claim:
	Is the claim supported by sufficient evidence? Yes No

Author's Claim:	Evidence to Support the Claim:
	Is the claim supported by sufficient evidence? Yes No

Author's Claim:	Evidence to Support the Claim:
	Is the claim supported by sufficient evidence? Yes No

After identifying the claims and evidence presented by this author, what argument do you think she or he is making?

After evaluating the evidence that supports each claim, is the overall argument supported by sufficient evidence? Explain why or why not.

Mid-Unit Assessment

Tracing and Evaluating an Argument: Video about DDT

Name: _____

Date: _____

I can identify the speaker's argument and specific claims in a video about DDT. (RI.6.8)

I can determine whether the speaker's argument and claims are supported by evidence. (SL.6.3)

After evaluating the evidence that supports each claim, is the overall argument supported by sufficient evidence? Explain why or why not.

_____

_____

_____

_____

_____

_____

Multiple choice: Circle the best answer for each of the following questions.

1. The evidence used by the speaker in this video helps support the position that birds at the top of the food chain have been harmed the most by DDT. The speaker does this by:

    a. Sharing a story about DDT and how it affected animals, particularly birds

    b. Stating claims about birds and their environment and using evidence to support the claims

    c. Explaining the build-up of DDT in the environment

2. The speaker states that bio-magnification, also called bio-accumulation, caused DDT to build up in the food chain. How does the video help the viewer understand this process?

    a. Gives facts and statistics

    b. Shows drawings of smaller fish to larger fish and birds

    c. Tells a true story

Glossary

Name: _____

Date: _____

Video about DDT	
bio-magnification	*n.* making something greater (as a pesticide) in a living organism
bio-accumulation	*n.* the gradual increasing of a substance (as a pesticide) in a living organism

"Rachel Carson: Sounding the Alarm on Pollution" article	
pollution	*n.* the action or process of making land, water, air, etc. dirty and not safe or suitable to use
conservation	*n.* the protection of animals, plants, and natural resources
synthetic	*adj.* made by combining different substances; not natural
aerial	*adj.* performed in the air or by using an airplane

Rachel Carson: Sounding the Alarm on Pollution
By Robert W. Peterson

Rachel Carson was a small, soft-spoken scientist.

She also was one of the towering Green Giants of the 20th century.

Her Book Changed Our World

Her 1962 book, "Silent Spring," was probably the most influential work on conservation ever written. It made Americans think hard about pollution of the environment. It led to strict controls on synthetic pesticides.

Rachel Carson was a marine biologist. She already had published three excellent books about the sea and its creatures. All were best sellers. They combined sound science with good writing.

Deadly Chemicals

The purpose of "Silent Spring" was to raise public alarm about chemical pesticides, especially one called DDT, which was introduced in 1939.

In the 1940s, the chemical industry developed many related pesticides. The pesticides saved farmers and gardeners time and money because they made it easier to control insects and weeds. By the mid-1950s, half a billion pounds of pesticides were being spread over fields and gardens each year.

The trouble was that some chemicals hurt not only insects and weeds, but also birds, mammals and fish. Some scientists said the chemicals hurt people too. Others had written about the danger before Rachel Carson wrote "Silent Spring," but few people paid attention.

Thousands of Dead Fish

By 1960, though, the evidence was clear. Fish had died by the tens of thousands when orchards near lakes were sprayed with pesticides. Thousands of birds had been doomed by aerial spraying of woodlands.

Rachel Carson's "Silent Spring" fairly shouted: "Whoa! Look what we're doing!" She did *not* oppose the use of all pesticides. But she wrote, "We have allowed these chemicals to be used with little or no advance investigation of their effect on soil, water, wildlife, and man himself."

Parts of the book began appearing in *The New Yorker* magazine in 1962. Rachel's message made for a noisy summer. It was attacked by the chemical industry, food companies, and some government agencies. They said the book was scientifically unsound. They dismissed her as a "nature nut," "food faddist," and "just a bird watcher."

Mild-Mannered but Tough

Rachel was quiet and mild-mannered, but she was also tough-minded. She stood up to all criticism and enjoyed the praise that came from many scientists who knew about pesticides.

In the following years, DDT and 11 other chemical pesticides Rachel had warned about were banned or tightly restricted. By the time of her death in 1964, her name was a household word.

A Writer at Age 10

Rachel Carson had come a long way from her childhood in a small town near Pittsburgh, Pa.

She had learned to love nature as a young girl. Her mother could not bear to kill a living thing, and so Rachel had to catch insects that got into the house and release them outside.

Rachel's first published story appeared in *St. Nicholas,* a children's magazine, when she was only 10 years old. She decided to become a writer, but in college she had to take a science course. She chose biology—and liked it. That was the start of a career that joined science with literature.

By the time she had published her third best seller on the sea, Rachel Carson was famous. People were ready to listen to her scary message in "Silent Spring." It changed how they thought about the earth— and also how they treated it.

Carson at a Glance

Born: May 27, 1907, at Springdale, Pa.; died April 14, 1964.

Legacy for the Earth: She put a spotlight on environmental pollution.

For Further Reading: "Sea and Earth: The Life of Rachel Carson," by Philip Sterling; "Rachel Carson" by Carol. B. Gartner.

"Future historians may well be amazed by our distorted sense of proportion. How could intelligent beings seek to control a few unwanted species by a method that contaminated the entire environment and brought the threat of disease and death even to their own kind? Yet this is what we have done."—*Rachel Carson's warning in* "Silent Spring"

Joe Ciardiello www.joeciardiello.com

"Rachel Carson: Sounding the Alarm on Pollution" by Robert W. Peterson, published in *Boys' Life Magazine*, August 1994, pages 38–39. From the series "Green Giants: Heroes of the Environment."

Mid-Unit Assessment

Tracing and Evaluating an Argument: "Rachel Carson: Sound the Alarm on Pollution"

Name: _____

Date: _____

I can identify the author's argument and specific claims in a text. (RI.6.8)

I can determine whether the author's argument and claims are supported by evidence. (RI.6.8)

Title of the Article: "Rachel Carson: Sounding the Alarm on Pollution"	
Directions: Read the article. After you have read it, write down what you have identified as the argument in the text. Write down a specific claim from the article. Then write what evidence was given to support the claim. Decide if the evidence did a good job supporting the claim.	
Author's Argument:	
Author's Claim:	**Evidence to Support the Claim:** **Is the claim supported by sufficient evidence?** **Yes No**

After evaluating the evidence that supports each claim, is the overall argument supported by sufficient evidence? Explain why or why not.

_____

_____

_____

_____

_____

_____

_____

_____

_____

EXPEDITIONARY
LEARNING

Learning from Frightful's Perspective

Chapter 8

Name: _____

Date: _____

Chapter 8: "Hunger Is Frightful's Teacher" **Words I Found Difficult:** **Glossary:** cote—*noun:* a small shed or coop for small animals transformer—*noun:* a device that transfers electric energy from one alternating-circuit current to one or more other circuits, either increasing (stepping up) or reducing (stepping down) the voltage raptors—*noun:* any bird of prey; examples of raptors include owls, eagles, falcons, hawks, and vultures	**Focus question:** What does Jon teach Frightful? How does he teach her this lesson? Use evidence from this chapter to support your thoughts.
	My thoughts: / **Evidence from the text:**

Sam Interacts with Frightful Cascading Consequences Chart

Name: _____

Date: _____

Sam Interacts with
Frightful

Sam Does Not Interact with Frightful Cascading Consequences Chart

Name: _____

Date: _____

Sam Does Not
Interacts with
Frightful

EXPEDITIONARY
LEARNING

Fishbowl Assessment

Scoring	
Consistently Demonstrated	2 points
Somewhat Demonstrated	1 point
Not Demonstrated	0 points

Assessment	1 Asks Questions to Understand Different Perspectives	2 References Text and Refers to Evidence	3 Advocates Persuasively	4 Responds to Questions with Details That Contribute to the Topic	Total Points
Name					

EXPEDITIONARY
LEARNING

Fishbowl Discussion Partner Scoring Log

Name: _____

Partner's Name: _____

Date: _____

Effective Fishbowl participants:

- Come well prepared with cascading consequences charts.
- Say things that show they understand the information from the resources.
- Say things that connect with what other participants are saying.
- Use claims and evidence from the resources to support ideas.
- Use good eye contact, appropriate voice level, and body language.
- Listen actively and avoid side conversations.
- Encourage others to speak.
- Ask questions to understand others' perspectives.

Identify one success and one goal for your partner.

1. Number of questions or comments made (Tally)

   _____

2. Number of claims and evidence from the resources (Tally)

   _____

3. How was the quality of his or her questions or comments? (Is he or she knowledgeable?)

   Excellent   Good   Fair   Poor   Unacceptable

4. How was his or her eye contact, voice level, and body language?

   Excellent   Good   Fair   Poor   Unacceptable

5. Did he or she follow good partnership manners? (Respect others' comments, listen attentively, no side conversations.)

   All of the time   Most of the time   Some of the time   Not at all

6. Did your partner meet his or her goals for the Fishbowl discussion?

   All of the time   Most of the time   Some of the time   Not at all

Reflection

Two successes:

_____

_____

_____

_____

_____

One goal:

_____

_____

_____

_____

_____

EXPEDITIONARY
LEARNING

Exit Ticket

Cascading Consequences Chart and Fishbowl Discussion

Name: _____

Date: _____

Share three things students need to do to be successful in a Fishbowl discussion.

1.

2.

3.

Share two important things to remember about sharing information on the cascading consequences chart.

1.

2.

Share one question you have about the Fishbowl discussion or the cascading consequences chart.

1.

Learning from Frightful's Perspective

Chapter 9

Name: _____

Date: _____

Chapter 9: "Frightful Finds Sam" **Words I Found Difficult:** **Glossary:** girder—*noun:* a strong beam used to build buildings, bridges, etc. imprint—*verb:* to cause (something) to stay in your mind or memory incubate—*verb:* to sit on eggs so that they will be kept warm and will hatch scrape—*noun:* the nest of a bird consisting of a usually shallow depression in the ground mottled—*adjective:* marked with colored spots or areas pores—*noun:* tiny openings especially in an animal or plant; one by which matter passes through a membrane	**Focus question:** Where does Frightful build her nest? What two important events happen at Frightful's nest? How do these events show the consequences of human interaction and the natural world? Use evidence from the text to support your thinking.
	My thoughts: / **Evidence from the text:**

Summer Resorts among the Catskills

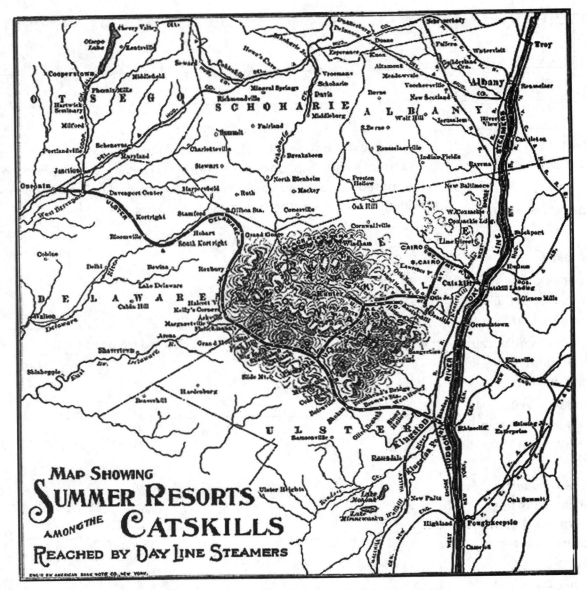

Wikipedia. "Summer Resorts Among the Catskills." December 30, 2011.
http://upload.wikimedia.org/wikipedia/en/2/2c/Udmap.jpg. Public Domain.

Benefits of DDT Cascading Consequences Chart

Name: _____

Date: _____

Resources:

Article: "The Exterminator" (EX)

Video: "John Stossel – DDT" (V-JS)

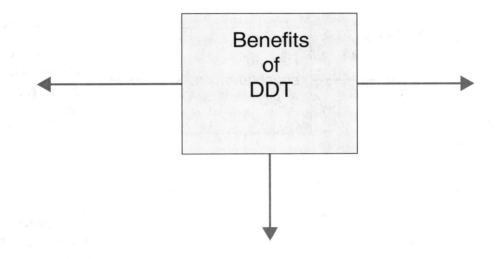

Harmful Consequences of DDT Cascading Consequences Chart

Name: _____

Date: _____

Resources:

Article: "Welcome Back" (EX)

Video: "DDT – Dichloro-diphenyl-trichloroethane" (V-DDT)

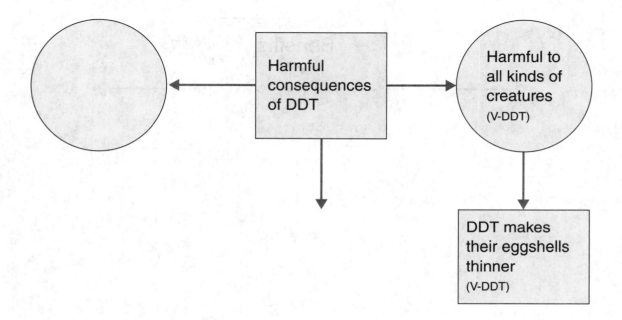

Fishbowl Feedback Checklist

Name: _____

Partner's Name: _____

Date: _____

_____ Well prepared with cascading consequences charts and resources.

_____ Made comments using claims and evidence from the resources.

_____ Used good eye contact and good voice level.

_____ Asked questions or encouraged others to speak.

Exit Ticket

Fishbowl Successes and Fishbowl Goals

Name: _____

Date: _____

Think about what you did well in the Fishbowl discussion. Write two things that were successful.

_____

_____

_____

_____

_____

_____

Think about what you would like to improve for your participation in the Fishbowl discussion. Write two goals that you would like to work on.

_____

_____

_____

_____

_____

_____

_____

EXPEDITIONARY
LEARNING

Learning from Frightful's Perspective
Chapter 10

Name: _____

Date: _____

Chapter 10: "There Are Eggs and Trouble"	**Focus question:** Frightful lays three eggs in her nest on the Delhi bridge. Explain how she and 426 care for their eggs. Later, in Chapter 10, human impact threatens Frightful and her eggs. Describe what threatens Frightful's eggs and how Sam helps Frightful through this challenge.	
Words I Found Difficult: **Glossary:** chalazas—*noun:* either of two spiral bands in the white of a bird's egg that extends from the yolk and attaches to opposite ends of the lining membrane albumen—*noun:* the white of an egg clutch—*noun:* the act of grasping, holding, or restraining trance—*noun:* the state of being lost in thought conservation—*noun:* a careful preservation and protection of something; *especially* planned management of a natural resource to prevent exploitation, destruction, or neglect	**My thoughts:**	**Evidence from the text:**

Interpreting Charts and Graphs Graphic Organizer

Name: _____

Date: _____

Issue: Do the benefits of DDT outweigh its harmful consequences?

Graph/Chart/Map Title:

_____

What is the graph telling the reader?	Where does it take place?

Who is affected?	When did it happen?

Interpreting Charts and Graphs Anchor Chart

Using DDT caused: _____

Not using DDT caused: _____

What are the benefits?	What are the harmful consequences?

Increases in Malaria for Countries in South America, 1993–1995

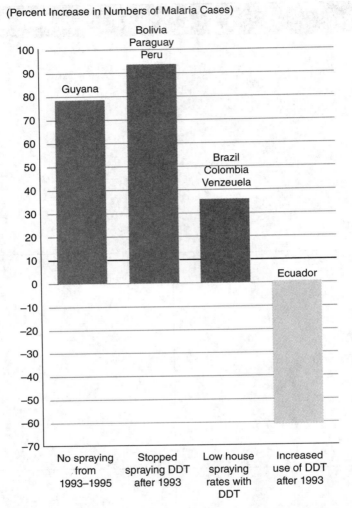

(Percent Increase in Numbers of Malaria Cases)

Roberts, Donald R. et al. Figure 7 from "DDT, Global Strategies and a Malaria Control Crisis in South America." Graph. Emerging Infectious Diseases. July–Sept. 1997. Web. wwwnc.cdc.gov/eid/article/3/3/pdfs/97-0305.pdf

EXPEDITIONARY
LEARNING

DDT in Human Body Fat in United States

Table 25.2. Average levels of DDT in human body fat for individuals living in the United States, 1942–1978 (PPM, mg/g fat).

Year	DDT level	Year	DDT level
1942	0	1970	11.6
1950	5.3	1972	9.2
1954–56	11.7	1974	6.7
1961–62	12.6	1976	5.5
1962–63	10.3	1978	4.8
1968	12.5	–	–

Sources: Ehrlich, P. R., Ehrlich, A. H., and Holdren, J. P., *Ecoscience, Population, Resources, Environment,* W. H. Freeman and Co., San Francisco, 1977, and Marco, G. J., Hollingworth, R. M., and Durham, W., *Silent Spring Revisited,* American Chemical Society, Washington, D.C., page 119, 1987.

DDT Bad, Malaria Much Worse

Monday, September 24, 2007

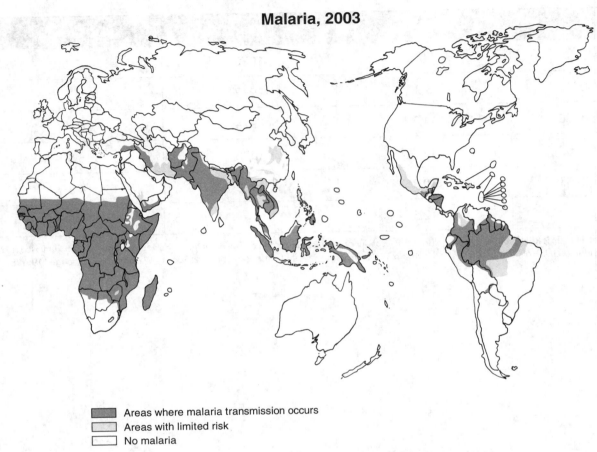

Malaria, 2003

Areas where malaria transmission occurs
Areas with limited risk
No malaria

"Malaria, 2003." Map. From World Health Organization. Blonde Sagacity. 2003.
http://mobyrebuttal.blogspot.com/2007/09/ddt-bad-malaria-much-worse.html

Malaria Trends in South Africa

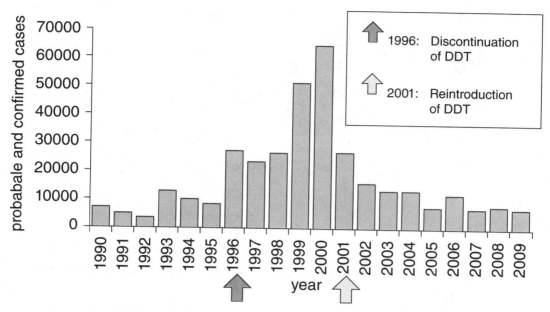

http://origin-ars.els-cdn.com/content/image/1-s2.0-S0048969712004767-gr1.jpg

DDT and Malaria in Ceylon

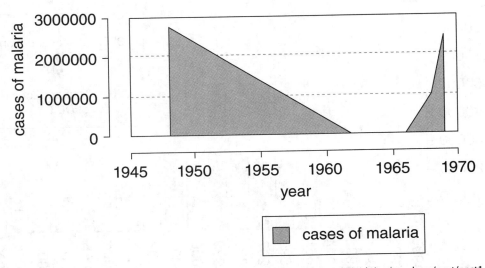

"DDT and Malaria in Ceylon." Graph. Cruising Chemistry. Web. www.chem.duke.edu/~jds/cruise_chem/pest/pest1.html

Bio Magnification in Lake Kariba, Africa

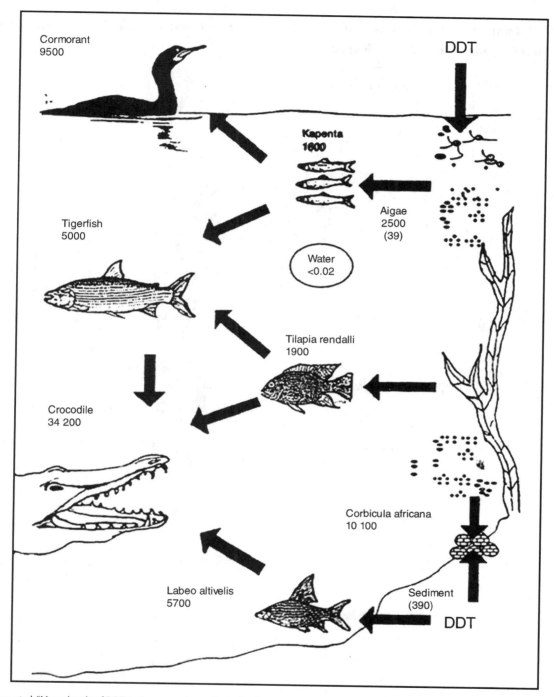

Berg, Hakan et al. "Mean levels of DDT in the ecosystem of Lake Kariba." Graphic from "DDT and Other Insecticides in the Lake Kariba Ecosystem, Zimbabwe." AMBIO. November 1992, page 449.

Changes in the Thickness of Eggshells

Figure 25.5. Changes in the thickness of eggshells of the peregrine falcon in Britain. The arrow shows when DDT first came into widespread use.

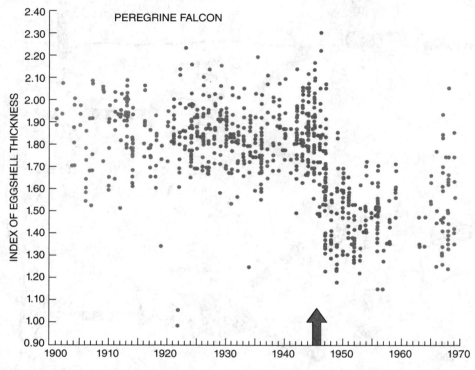

Ehrlich, P.R. et al. "Changes in the thickness of eggshells of the peregrine falcon in Britain." *Ecoscience, Population, Resources, Environment.* W. H. Freeman and Co. San Francisco. 1977.

DDT in Breast Milk

Time Trend Examples

Sweden has excellent data from breast milk monitoring studies spanning more than 30 years. DDT levels in breast milk continuously declined from 1967 through 1997. The use of DDT was severely restricted in Sweden in 1970 and completely banned in 1975. Figure 1 shows the marked decrease in the average concentrations of DDT found in Swedish women's breast milk.

Figure 1

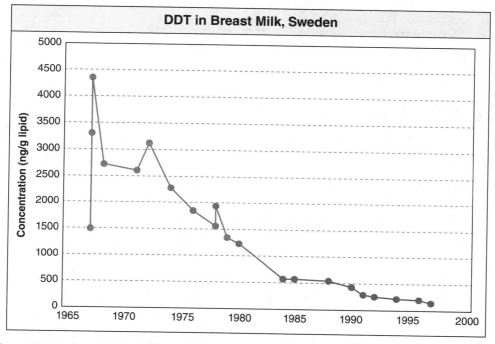

"DDT in Breast Milk, Sweden and DDT in Breast Milk, West Germany." Graph. National Resources Defense Council. New York. 2005. Web. www.nrdc.org/breastmilk/ddt.asp

Germany has also witnessed a rapid decline in average concentrations of DDT in breast milk. Between 1969 and 1995, detectable residue levels decreased 81 percent. DDT was banned in Germany in 1972. However, trend data in Germany is difficult to assess on a national basis because East and West Germany had different use patterns before reunification. Figure 2 shows the declining trend of DDT residues in the former West Germany. The decline has been similar in the former eastern state, but the data are far less complete. In addition, the average concentrations in East Germany were much higher during the 1970s, with the highest detected residue levels (~11,500 µg/kg DDT in milk fat) recorded in Greifswald, East Germany, in 1971.

Figure 2

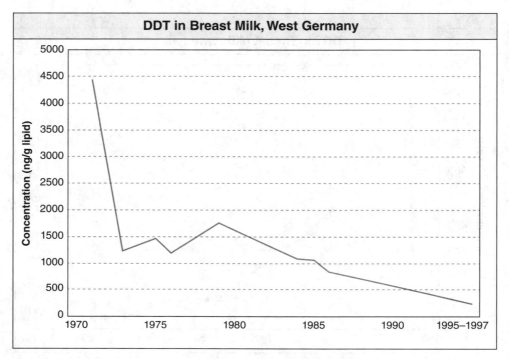

"DDT in Breast Milk, Sweden and DDT in Breast Milk, West Germany." Graph. National Resources Defense Council. New York. 2005. Web. www.nrdc.org/breastmilk/ddt.asp

Learning from Frightful's Perspective
Chapter 11

Name: _____

Date: _____

| Chapter 11: "The Kids Are Heard"

Words I Found Difficult:

Glossary:

embryos—*noun:* humans or animals in the early stages of development before they are born or hatched

protesters—*noun:* people who show or express strong disagreement with or disapproval of something

detour—*noun:* the act of going or traveling to a place along a way that is different from the usual or planned way

hatching—*verb:* coming out of an egg; being born by coming out of an egg | **Focus question:** Efforts are being made by the kids in Delhi to stop bridge construction while Frightful and 426's eggs hatch. Use evidence from **c**hapter 11 to describe at least three things the kids are doing to get people's attention to help Frightful and 426. |
| | **My thoughts:** / **Evidence from the text:** |

Resource Reference Sheet
Benefits of DDT Cascading Consequences Chart

Name: _____

Date: _____

Resources

Articles
"The Exterminator" (EX)

"Double Whammy" (EX/D.W.)

"Public Fear" (EX/P.F.)

"Seriously Sick" (EX/S.S.)

"Killer Genes" (EX/K.G.)

Video
"John Stossel – DDT" (V-J.S.)

Graphs and Charts
"DDT Bad, Malaria much worse" (world map)

"Malaria Trends in South Africa" (graph)

"Increases in Malaria for Countries in South America, 1993–1995" (graph)

"DDT and Malaria in Ceylon" (graph)

Resource Reference Sheet

Harmful Consequences of DDT Cascading Consequences Chart

Name: _____

Date: _____

Resources

Articles

"Welcome Back" (W.B.)

"Rachel Carson: Sounding the Alarm on Pollution" (R.C.)

Video

"DDT – Dichloro-diphenyl-trichloroethane" (V-DDT)

Graphs, Tables, Charts, Diagrams, Maps

"Lake Kariba, Africa DDT Levels" (diagram)

"DDT in Human Body Fat in United States" (table)

"DDT in Breast Milk" (graph)

"Changes in the Thickness of Eggshells" (graph)

Fishbowl Note-Catcher

Name: _____

Date: _____

Process *(Identify what inner- and outer-circle students do.)*	Purpose *(Why is this done?)*
Materials Inner circle: Outer circle:	
Claims and Evidence	
Resources	
Voice and Eye Contact	
Discussion and Questions	

Fishbowl Assessment

Scoring	
Consistently Demonstrated	2 points
Somewhat Demonstrated	1 point
Not Demonstrated	0 points

Assessment	1 Asks Questions to Understand Different Perspectives	2 References Text and Refers to Evidence	3 Advocates Persuasively	4 Responds to Questions with Details That Contribute to the Topic	Total Points
Name					

EXPEDITIONARY
LEARNING

End-of-Unit 1 Assessment

Fishbowl Discussion: Do the Benefits of DDT Outweigh Its Harmful Consequences?

Students in the inner circle discuss.

Scoring	
Consistently Demonstrated	2 points
Somewhat Demonstrated	1 point
Not Demonstrated	0 points

Assessment	1 Asks Questions to Understand Different Perspectives	2 References Text and Refers to Evidence	3 Advocates Persuasively	4 Responds to Questions with Details That Contribute to the Topic	Total Points
Name					

Exit Ticket

Two Stars and One Step

Name: _____

Date: _____

Stars:

_____

_____

_____

_____

_____

Steps:

_____

_____

_____

_____

_____

Learning from Frightful's Perspective

Chapter 12

Name: _____

Date: _____

Chapter 12: "There Are Three"	**Focus question:** When Flip Pearson and Dr. Werner take the eyases, Molly wants a chance to see them. What does Molly notice when Flip allows her to look in the bag?	
Words I Found Difficult:		
Glossary:		
horizontal—*adjective:* positioned from side to side rather than up and down; parallel to the ground	**My thoughts:**	**Evidence from the Text:**
vertical—*adjective:* positioned up and down rather than from side to side; going straight up		
torrents—*noun:* large amounts of water that move very quickly in one direction		
morsel—*noun:* a small piece of food		

Credibility Checklist

Name: _____

Date: _____

Source Information	Most Credible	Fairly Credible	Least Credible
Author	Expert in the field	Educated on topic	Little or no information about the author
Date	Recently published or revised	Outdated	No date listed
Source Type	Official websites, institutional sites, academic journals, reputable news sources	Published material	Unfamiliar websites
Publisher	Publisher's relationship to the topic is balanced or neutral	Publisher is sponsored by a trusted source	Clearly biased or favoring a position for a purpose

Assessing Sources

Name: _____

Date: _____

When you find a text you might use for research, assess it first by asking these questions.

1. Assess the Text's Accessibility

- Am I able to read and comprehend the text easily?
- Do I have adequate background knowledge to understand the terminology, information, and ideas in the text?

2. Assess the Text's Credibility

- Is the author an expert on the topic?
- Is the purpose to inform?
- Is the purpose to persuade?
- Is the purpose to sell?
- Is the tone convincing?
- Does the text have specific facts and details to support the ideas?

3. Assess the Text's Relevance

- Does the text have information that helps me answer my research question? Is it information that I don't have already?
- How does the information in the text relate to other sources I have found?

Informed by "Assessing Sources," designed by Odell Education.

Rachel Carson: Sounding the Alarm on Pollution

By Robert W. Peterson

Rachel Carson was a small, soft-spoken scientist.

She also was one of the towering Green Giants of the 20th century.

Her Book Changed Our World

Her 1962 book, "Silent Spring," was probably the most influential work on conservation ever written. It made Americans think hard about pollution of the environment. It led to strict controls on synthetic pesticides.

Rachel Carson was a marine biologist. She already had published three excellent books about the sea and its creatures. All were best sellers. They combined sound science with good writing.

Deadly Chemicals

The purpose of "Silent Spring" was to raise public alarm about chemical pesticides, especially one called DDT, which was introduced in 1939.

In the 1940s, the chemical industry developed many related pesticides. The pesticides saved farmers and gardeners time and money because they made it easier to control insects and weeds. By the mid-1950s, half a billion pounds of pesticides were being spread over fields and gardens each year.

The trouble was that some chemicals hurt not only insects and weeds, but also birds, mammals and fish. Some scientists said the chemicals hurt people too. Others had written about the danger before Rachel Carson wrote "Silent Spring," but few people paid attention.

Thousands of Dead Fish

By 1960, though, the evidence was clear. Fish had died by the tens of thousands when orchards near lakes were sprayed with pesticides. Thousands of birds had been doomed by aerial spraying of woodlands.

Rachel Carson's "Silent Spring" fairly shouted: "Whoa! Look what we're doing!" She did *not* oppose the use of all pesticides. But she wrote, "We have allowed these chemicals to be used with little or no advance investigation of their effect on soil, water, wildlife, and man himself."

Parts of the book began appearing in *The New Yorker* magazine in 1962. Rachel's message made for a noisy summer. It was attacked by the chemical industry, food companies, and some government agencies. They said the book was scientifically unsound. They dismissed her as a "nature nut," "food faddist," and "just a bird watcher."

Mild-Mannered but Tough

Rachel was quiet and mild-mannered, but she was also tough-minded. She stood up to all criticism and enjoyed the praise that came from many scientists who knew about pesticides.

In the following years, DDT and 11 other chemical pesticides Rachel had warned about were banned or tightly restricted. By the time of her death in 1964, her name was a household word.

A Writer at Age 10

Rachel Carson had come a long way from her childhood in a small town near Pittsburgh, Pa.

She had learned to love nature as a young girl. Her mother could not bear to kill a living thing, and so Rachel had to catch insects that got into the house and release them outside.

Rachel's first published story appeared in *St. Nicholas,* a children's magazine, when she was only 10 years old. She decided to become a writer, but in college she had to take a science course. She chose biology—and liked it. That was the start of a career that joined science with literature.

By the time she had published her third best seller on the sea, Rachel Carson was famous. People were ready to listen to her scary message in "Silent Spring." It changed how they thought about the earth— and also how they treated it.

"Rachel Carson: Sounding the Alarm on Pollution" by Robert W. Peterson, published in *Boys' Life Magazine,* August 1994, pages 38–39. From the series "Green Giants: Heroes of the Environment."

Rachel Carson: Environmentalist and Writer

"Man's way is not always best."

By Kathy Wilmore

When you hear the world "revolutionary," what image comes to mind? An angry, wild-eyed man toting a machine gun, perhaps? Or do you look back in history to see someone like George Washington or Paul Revere? How about the environmentalist and writer Rachel Carson? She may not look the part, but Rachel Carson was a true revolutionary. Her work as a writer and scientist stirred people up and helped launch a new age of environmental awareness in the United States.

In 1962, Carson published *Silent Spring,* her fourth book on nature. It had an almost fairy-tale beginning: "There once was a town in the heart of America where all life seemed to live in harmony with its surroundings."

However, something in that town went horribly wrong. Sickness and death appeared everywhere: among flowers and trees, cattle and sheep, even humans. "There was a strange stillness," wrote Carson. "The birds, for example—where had they gone? . . . The few birds seen anywhere . . . trembled violently and could not fly. It was a spring without voices. On the mornings that had once throbbed with the dawn chorus of . . . (many) bird voices there was now no sound: only silence lay over the fields and woods and marsh."

Carson went on to explain the cause of that eerie silence: "Pesticides" (insect-killing chemicals) had gotten into the water, air, and soil and were killing or sickening all sorts of creatures—including humans. "Can anyone believe," she wrote, "it is possible to lay down such a barrage of poisons on the surface of the earth without making it unfit for all life? They should not be called "insecticides" [insect killers] but biocides [life killers]."

If we are not more careful with the chemicals we use, warned Carson, the nightmarish silence described in *Silent Spring* could come true.

Anything but Silence

The reaction to Carson's book was anything but silence. It caused such an uproar that a *New York Times* headline declared: SILENT SPRING IS NOW NOISY SUMMER.

Chemical manufacturers were furious with Carson. They ran ads telling Americans to ignore *Silent Spring*. They questioned Carson's abilities as a scientist, calling her a hysterical fanatic. Pesticides, they said, are perfectly safe—don't worry about a thing.

But Americans did worry. The White House and the Congress were flooded with letters from anxious citizens demanding that something be done. President John F. Kennedy called for a special committee of scientists to investigate Carson's claims. Congress also formed an investigation committee.

The soft-spoken Carson would rather have spent her days on the rocky coast of Maine, where she did much of her research as a marine biologist (scientist who studies sea life). But the storm of debate surrounding her book and its critics pulled her into the limelight.

Coming to Terms with Nature

In defending her research, Carson told Americans to think for themselves. Who had the most to win or lose if she turned out to be correct? "As you listen to the present controversy about pesticides," said Carson, "I recommend that you ask yourself: Who speaks? And why?"

The main thing to consider, she said, is our future. What kind of world do we want to leave our children? "I deeply believe," Carson told Congress, "that we in this generation must come to terms with nature."

Carson's ideas may not seem revolutionary today. But back in 1962, few people were familiar with such terms as pollution and ecology and environmental awareness. U.S. industries were constantly coming out with useful and exciting new products, but few people stopped to think if there could be negative side effects to any of them. Humans did what was convenient for them. Nature to most people was something that just took care of itself.

A Message to Remember

President Kennedy's commission supported Carson's warnings. So did other government studies. Armed with such new data and the public outcry, Congress began passing laws to ban or control the use of potentially dangerous pesticides. It also called for more careful testing of chemicals' side effects. In 1970, Congress established the Environmental Protection Agency (EPA) to reduce and control pollution of water, air, and soil. Rachel Carson did not live to see all of this happen. She died of cancer in 1964.

What about us? Can we avoid the "silent spring" that Carson predicted? In the 31 years since *Silent Spring* first appeared, people have grown far more aware of our impact on the environment. But we still use many potentially deadly chemicals.

A 1993 *New York Times* article says that "68 pesticide ingredients [not in use] have been determined to cause cancer. One out of every 10 community drinking-water wells contains pesticides . . . Farmers exposed to "herbicides" [weed killers] have a six times greater risk than others of contracting certain cancers. Children in homes using pesticides are seven time as likely to develop childhood leukemia [a form of cancer]."

"There remains, in this space-age universe," wrote Rachel Carson, "the possibility that man's way is not always best." We would do well to remember her warning.

Wilmore, Kathy. "Rachel Carson: Environmentalist and Writer." *Scholastic Junior Magazine.* 2013. www.scholastic.com/browse/article.jsp?id=4964

Malaria Carrying Mosquito Crash Lands Due to His Insecticide

By Adam Allie

Paul Müller was a chemist who made a discovery that led to the rapid decrease of many dangerous insect transmitted diseases. He did this by finding one of the most effective and controversial pesticides in history. It has been found to be effective in killing the mosquito, which spreads malaria; the louse, which spreads typhus; the flea, which spreads the plague; and the sandfly, which spreads tropical diseases. It was a main factor in complete elimination of malaria in Europe, the U.S., Japan, and Australia. This pesticide is called dichloro-diphenyl-trichloroethane, more commonly known as DDT.

Müller was an independent scientist often referred to in the labs as a lone wolf, or as his daughter related, an Eigenbrotler—someone "who makes his own bread." Two events occurred that influenced his research into insecticides. The first was a severe food shortage in Switzerland, which demonstrated the need for better insect control of crops. The second event was the Russian typhus epidemic, the largest typhus epidemic in history. Müller, with his background in chemistry and botany, found himself both motivated and prepared for the challenge.

He worked for J.R. Geigy (which eventually became today's drug giant Novartis), developing tanning methods for protecting clothes from insects, and a safe seed disinfectant that wasn't based on poisonous mercury compounds, as was common in his era. After these successes, he decided to pursue the perfect synthetic insecticide. He absorbed all the information possible on the subject, came up with properties such an insecticide would exhibit, and set forth on his solitary quest to find it. After four years of work and 349 failures, in September of 1939, Müller placed a compound in his fly cage. After a short while the flies dropped and died. What he had found was DDT.

In 1948, Paul Müller was awarded the Nobel Prize in Medicine, despite the fact that he was neither a doctor nor a medical researcher, but rather a chemist. Such recognition speaks volumes about the world's perception of the benefits of DDT in preventing human disease. Later, due to overuse, questions began to surface about its impact on nature. Then environmentalists rallied against it, which culminated in the U.S. Environment[al] Protection Agency banning DDT in 1972. Soon, most other countries also banned its use. Environmentalists and public health advocates remained polarized for decades over DDT. It wasn't until September, 2006, that the World Health Organization reversed its stance and admitted DDT was at times the best insecticide to prevent malaria. As the years have passed, many on both sides of the debate are coming to realize proper limited use of DDT, on the inside walls of homes, can be effective and have virtually no impact on the environment.

Reprinted with permission from ScienceHeroes.com.

How DDT Harmed Hawks and Eagles
(Excerpt)

Pesticide DDT is a chemical compound that was a major factor in reducing the eagle and hawk populations around the world. Raptors were also hurt by other problems such as hunting and deforestation. The 1972 ban of DDT certainly contributed to the birds of prey's revival in the United States. It is important to understand how people have tracked and identified their progress. The modern day explosion of nesting pairs makes us realize the disastrous effects of synthetic pesticides.

The United States used DDT during the mid-1900s. During and after World War II (1939–1945), DDT was widely used as a synthetic pesticide to prevent insects from killing agricultural crops. It was popular with farmers, foresters, and domestic gardeners. The compound reached a global peak of 386 million pounds (175 million kilograms) in 1970. In 1959, the United States sprayed 79 million pounds (36 million kilograms) of DDT chemical compound.

The dangerous consequences of spraying synthetic pesticides were not realized until 1962. An American biologist, Rachel Carson, published *Silent Spring*. The public learned DDT caused cancer in people. The synthetic pesticide harmed eagles and other birds of prey populations. Bald eagles were threatened with extinction in the lower 48 states. Finally, in June 1972, the U.S. Environmental Protection Agency (EPA) banned DDT use in the United States. Recently as May 23, 2001, DDT pesticide use was limited worldwide at the Stockholm Convention.

Birds of prey species badly affected by synthetic pesticide use included: peregrine falcons, sharp-shinned hawks, Cooper's hawks, Eurasian sparrow hawks, osprey, bald eagles, white-tailed eagles, brown pelicans, and herons.

The eagle needs rich soil and its fertility. Grass cannot grow on deteriorated soil. A diminishing rabbit population hurts eagle populations. DDT contaminated many soils and plants. Mice stored the poisonous particles in their fatty tissues. Hawks consumed numerous mice, and their numbers declined because of DDT poisoning.

Bald eagle populations decreased as low as 500 nesting pairs in the lower 48 states. Some bald eagles were poisoned because their fish ingested synthetic pesticides. The 1972 DDT ban and the 1973 Endangered Species Act, helped reverse a dismal trend. The lower 48 states noticed an increase of over 5,000 nesting pairs. 70,000 bald eagles inhabit North America.

In 2007, the American bald eagle was taken off the endangered species list in Wisconsin. In 1973, the bald eagle inhabited 108 territories in the state. Those territories rose to 1,150 breeding pairs in 2010. Half of the eagle population nest on privately owned land. It makes it important for Wisconsin citizens to understand the importance of protecting eagles.

Author:

Gil Valo (interested citizen)

Date:

July 26, 2007

Source:

www.actforlibraries.org/how-ddt-harmed-hawks-and-eagles

Publisher:

www.helium.com

Valo, Gil. "How DDT harmed hawks and eagles." Helium. 26 July 2011. Web. www.actforlibraries.org/how-ddt-harmed-hawks-and-eagles/.

EXPEDITIONARY
LEARNING

A New Home for DDT
(Excerpt)

By Donald Roberts

Bethesda, Md.

DDT, the miracle insecticide turned environmental bogeyman, is once again playing an important role in public health. In the malaria-plagued regions of Africa, where mosquitoes are becoming resistant to other chemicals, DDT is now being used as an indoor repellent. Research that I and my colleagues recently conducted shows that DDT is the most effective pesticide for spraying on walls, because it can keep mosquitoes from even entering the room.

The news may seem surprising, as some mosquitoes worldwide are already resistant to DDT. But we've learned that even mosquitoes that have developed an immunity to being directly poisoned by DDT are still repelled by it.

Malaria accounts for nearly 90 percent of all deaths from vector-borne disease globally. And it is surging in Africa, surpassing AIDS as the biggest killer of African children under age 5.

From the 1940s onward, DDT was used to kill agricultural pests and disease-carrying insects because it was cheap and lasted longer than other insecticides. DDT helped much of the developed world, including the United States and Europe, eradicate malaria. Then in the 1970s, after the publication of Rachel Carson's *Silent Spring*, which raised concern over DDT's effects on wildlife and people, the chemical was banned in many countries. Birds, especially, were said to be vulnerable, and the chemical was blamed for reduced populations of bald eagles, falcons, and pelicans. Scientific scrutiny has failed to find conclusive evidence that DDT causes cancer or other health problems in humans.

Today, indoor DDT spraying to control malaria in Africa is supported by the World Health Organization; the Global Fund to Fight AIDS, Tuberculosis and Malaria; and the United States Agency for International Development.

It would be a mistake to think we could rely on DDT alone to fight mosquitoes in Africa. Fortunately, research aimed at developing new and better insecticides continues—thanks especially to the work of the international Innovative Vector Control Consortium. Until a suitable alternative is found, however, DDT remains the cheapest and most effective long-term malaria fighter we have.

Author:

Donald Roberts (professor emeritus of tropical medicine and board member of nonprofit Africa Fighting Malaria)

Source:

Opinion Editorial, *The New York Times*. www.nytimes.com/2007/08/20/opinion/20roberts.html?_r=0.\

Published:

The New York Times, August 20, 2007.

Roberts, Donald. "OP-ED CONTRIBUTOR; A New Home for DDT." *The New York Times. The New York Times,* 20 Aug. 2007. Web. www.nytimes.com/2007/08/20/opinion/20roberts.html?_r=1

DDT Use Should Be Last Resort in Malaria-Plagued Areas, Scientists Say
(Excerpts)

By Marla Cone, *Environmental Health News*

Monday, May 4, 2009

A panel of scientists recommended today that the spraying of DDT in malaria-plagued Africa and Asia should be greatly reduced because people are exposed in their homes to high levels that may cause serious health effects.

The scientists from the United States and South Africa said the insecticide, banned decades ago in most of the world, should only be used as a last resort in combating malaria.

The stance of the panel, led by a University of California epidemiologist, is likely to be controversial with public health officials. Use of DDT to fight malaria has been increasing since it was endorsed in 2006 by the World Health Organization and the President's Malaria Initiative, a U.S. aid program launched by former President Bush.

In many African countries, as well as India and North Korea, the pesticide is sprayed inside homes and buildings to kill mosquitoes that carry malaria.

Malaria is one of the world's most deadly diseases, each year killing about 880,000 people, mostly children in sub-Saharan Africa, according to the World Health Organization.

The 15 environmental health experts, who reviewed almost 500 health studies, concluded that DDT "should be used with caution, only when needed, and when no other effective, safe and affordable alternatives are locally available."

"We cannot allow people to die from malaria, but we also cannot continue using DDT if we know about the health risks," said Tiaan de Jager, a member of the panel who is a professor at the School of Health Systems & Public Health at the University of Pretoria in South Africa. "Safer alternatives should be tested first and if successful, DDT should be phased out without putting people at risk."

The scientists reported that DDT may have a variety of human health effects, including reduced fertility, genital birth defects, breast cancer, diabetes and damage to developing brains. Its metabolite, DDE, can block male hormones.

"Based on recent studies, we conclude that humans are exposed to DDT and DDE, that indoor residual spraying can result in substantial exposure and that DDT may pose a risk for human populations," the scientists wrote in their consensus statement, published online today in the journal *Environmental Health Perspectives*.

"We are concerned about the health of children and adults given the persistence of DDT and its active metabolites in the environment and in the body, and we are particularly concerned about the potential effects of continued DDT use on future generations."

In 2007, at least 3,950 tons of DDT were sprayed for mosquito control in Africa and Asia, according to a report by the United Nations Environment Programme.

"The volume is increasing slowly," said Hindrik Bouwman, a professor in the School of Environmental Sciences and Development at North-West University in Potchesfstroom, South Africa, who also served on the panel.

In South Africa, about 60 to 80 grams is sprayed in each household per year, Bouwman said.

Brenda Eskenazi, a University of California at Berkeley School of Public Health professor and lead author of the consensus statement, is concerned because the health of people inside the homes is not being monitored.

A 2007 study on male fertility is the only published research so far. Conducted in Limpopo, South Africa, by de Jager and his colleagues, the study found men in the sprayed homes had extremely high levels of DDT in their blood and that their semen volume and sperm counts were low.

"Clearly, more research is needed . . . but in the meantime, DDT should really be the last resort against malaria, rather than the first line of defense," Eskenazi said.

The pesticide accumulates in body tissues, particularly breast milk, and lingers in the environment for decades.

In the United States, beginning in the 1940s, large volumes of DDT were sprayed outdoors to kill mosquitoes and pests on crops. It was banned in 1972, after it built up in food chains, nearly wiping out bald eagles, pelicans and other birds.

Today's use differs greatly. In Africa, it is sprayed in much smaller quantities but people are directly exposed because it is sprayed on walls inside homes and other buildings.

Many health studies have been conducted in the United States, but on people who carry small traces of DDT in their bodies, not the high levels found in people in Africa.

"DDT is now used in countries where many of the people are malnourished, extremely poor and possibly suffering from immune-compromising diseases such as AIDS, which may increase their susceptibility to chemical exposures," said panel member Jonathan Chevrier, a University of California at Berkeley post-doctoral researcher in epidemiology and in environmental health sciences.

In 2001, more than 100 countries signed the Stockholm Convention, a United Nations treaty which sought to eliminate use of 12 persistent, toxic compounds, including DDT. Under the pact, use of the pesticide is allowed only for controlling malaria.

Since then, nine nations—Ethiopia, South Africa, India, Mauritius, Myanmar, Yemen, Uganda, Mozambique and Swaziland—notified the treaty's secretariat that they are using DDT. Five others—Zimbabwe, North Korea, Eritrea, Gambia, Namibia and Zambia—also reportedly are using it, and six others, including China, have reserved the right to begin using it, according to a January Stockholm Convention report.

"This is a global issue," Eskenazi said. "We need to enforce the Stockholm Convention and to have a plan for each country to phase out DDT, and if they feel they can't, good reason why other options cannot work."

Mexico, the rest of Central America and parts of Africa have combated malaria without DDT by using alternative methods, such as controlling stagnant ponds where mosquitoes breed and using bed nets treated with pyrethroid insecticides. But such efforts have been less successful in other places, particularly South Africa.

"We have a whole host of mosquito species and more than one parasite. The biology of the vectors is different and there is therefore no one-method-fits-all strategy, as is the case in Central America," Bouwman said.

For example, he said, some types of mosquitoes in South Africa breed in running water, which cannot be easily controlled.

"The area to be covered is also vast, and infrastructure in most areas is too little to allow environmental management on a sustainable basis," he said.

When a mosquito strain that had previously been eliminated returned to South Africa, it was resistant to the pyrethroid insecticides that had replaced DDT.

"The resulting increase in malaria cases and deaths was epidemic," Bouwman said. Cases soared from 4,117 in 1995 to 64,622 in 2000. "South Africa had to fall back on DDT, and still uses it in areas where other chemicals would have a risk of failure," he said.

The scientists also recommended study of possible health effects of pyrethroids and other alternatives for DDT. "The general thoughts are that if chemicals have a shorter half-life, like pyrethroids, they are less dangerous," Eskenazi said. "This may be true, but there are virtually no studies on the health effects in humans of the alternatives."

The panel convened in March, 2008, at Alma College in Michigan, near a Superfund site where DDT was produced at a chemical plant. Their goal was "to address the current and legacy implications of DDT production and use," according to their report.

Acknowledging that some areas remain dependent on DDT, they recommended monitoring of the spraying to ensure that usage guidelines are followed and improved application techniques.

"It is definitely not a matter of letting people die from malaria," de Jager said.

Author:

Marla Cone (editor in chief, *Environmental Health News*)

Source:

www.environmentalhealthnews.org/ehs/news/ddt-only-as-last-resort

Published:

Environmental Health News. May 4, 2009

Cone, Marla. "DDT Use Should be Last Resort in Malaria-Plagued Areas, Scientists Say." May 4, 2009. *Environmental Health News.* www.environmentalhealthnews.org/ehs/news/ddt-only-as-last-resort

Researcher's Notebook

Name: _____

Date: _____

Research question: Do the benefits of DDT outweigh its harmful consequences?

To plan for your research, think, talk, and write about the following questions:

1. What is a benefit?
2. What is a harmful consequence?
3. What important benefits of DDT do you already know about?
4. What important harmful consequences of DDT do you already know about?
5. What do you still wonder about DDT?

In this section, write a short, well-written paragraph describing the purpose for your research:

Research question: Do the benefits of DDT outweigh its harmful consequences?

Source Information	Claims/Central Ideas (*Paraphrase the benefits or harmful consequences.*)	Details/Evidence
Source 1:		
Source title:		
Author:		
Date:		
Source type (*newspaper article, book, website, video, etc.*):		
Credible? Yes / No (*Use your Credibility Checklist to guide you.*)		

Does this source help you refocus or refine your research question in any way? How?

What are new questions you would like answered before making your claim about DDT?

Research question: Do the benefits of DDT outweigh its harmful consequences?

Source Information	Claims/Central Ideas *(Paraphrase the benefits or harmful consequences.)*	Details/Evidence
Source 2:		
Source title:		
Author:		
Date:		
Source type *(newspaper article, book, website, video, etc.)*:		
Credible? Yes / No *(Use your Credibility Checklist to guide you.)*		

Does this source help you refocus or refine your research question in any way? How?

What are new questions you would like answered before making your claim about DDT?

Research question: Do the benefits of DDT outweigh its harmful consequences?

Source Information	Claims/Central Ideas (Paraphrase the benefits or harmful consequences.)	Details/Evidence
Source 3:		
Source title:		
Author:		
Date:		
Source type (newspaper article, book, website, video, etc.):		
Credible? Yes / No (Use your Credibility Checklist to guide you.)		

Does this source help you refocus or refine your research question in any way? How?

What are new questions you would like answered before making your claim about DDT?

Research question: Do the benefits of DDT outweigh its harmful consequences?

Source Information	Claims/Central Ideas (Paraphrase the benefits or harmful consequences.)	Details/Evidence
Source 4:		
Source title:		
Author:		
Date:		
Source type (newspaper article, book, website, video, etc.):		
Credible? Yes / No (Use your Credibility Checklist to guide you.)		

Does this source help you refocus or refine your research question in any way? How?

What are new questions you would like answered before making your claim about DDT?

Research question: Do the benefits of DDT outweigh its harmful consequences?

Source Information	Claims/Central Ideas *(Paraphrase the benefits or harmful consequences.)*	Details/Evidence
Source 5:		
Source title:		
Author:		
Date:		
Source type *(newspaper article, book, website, video, etc.):*		
Credible? Yes / No *(Use your Credibility Checklist to guide you.)*		

Does this source help you refocus or refine your research question in any way? How?

What are new questions you would like answered before making your claim about DDT?

Exit Ticket

"Rachel Carson: Environmentalist and Writer"

Paraphrasing an Excerpt from the Text

Name: _____

Date: _____

Directions: Paraphrase the quote from "Rachel Carson: Environmentalist and Writer."

"Anything but Silence

The reaction to Carson's book was anything but silence. It caused such an uproar that a *New York Times* headline declared: SILENT SPRING IS NOW NOISY SUMMER.

Chemical manufacturers were furious with Carson. They ran ads telling Americans to ignore *Silent Spring*. They questioned Carson's abilities as a scientist, calling her a hysterical fanatic. Pesticides, they said, are perfectly safe—don't worry about a thing."

_____

_____

_____

_____

_____

_____

_____

_____

_____

_____

_____

_____

_____

EXPEDITIONARY
LEARNING

Learning from Frightful's Perspective
Chapter 13

Name: _____

Date: _____

Chapter 13: "Sam Takes Charge" **Words I Found Difficult:** **Glossary:** poachers—*noun:* people who kill or take wild animals (as game or fish) illegally bivouac—*noun:* a temporary or casual shelter or lodging deluge—*noun:* a large amount of rain that suddenly falls in an area rivulets—*noun:* small streams of water or liquid endangered—*adjective:* used to describe a type of animal or plant that has become very rare and that could die out completely	**Focus question:** Flip Pearson and Dr. Werner took two of the eyases from the bridge for a reason. Why did the two men take the eyases?
	My thoughts:	**Evidence from the text:**

Comparing and Contrasting Authors' Presentation Graphic Organizer

Name: _____

Date: _____

Text 1 Title: "Rachel Carson: Environmentalist and Writer"	Compare and Contrast the Authors' Presentation	Text 2 Title: "Rachel Carson: Sounding the Alarm on Pollution"
How does the author **introduce** the article?	How are they similar? How are they different?	How does the author **introduce** the article?
What **claim** does the author make?	How are they similar? How are they different?	What **claim** does the author make?
What type of **evidence** does the author include?	How are they similar? How are they different?	What type of **evidence** does the author include?
How does the author use **text features** (photographs, graphs, diagrams, etc.)?	How are they similar? How are they different?	How does the author use **text features** (photographs, graphs, diagrams, etc.)?

Which article is more effective in its argument? Why?

_____

_____

_____

_____

_____

_____

_____

_____

_____

_____

_____

_____

_____

_____

_____

_____

_____

_____

_____

_____

Learning from Frightful's Perspective

Chapter 14

Name: _____

Date: _____

Chapter 14: "Sam Battles Bird Instincts"	**Focus question:** In what ways has Frightful changed from the beginning of the novel until now?	
Words I Found Difficult:		
Glossary:	**My thoughts:**	**Evidence from the text:**
eddy—*noun:* a circular current		
cupola—*noun:* a small structure built on top of a roof		
imprinted—*verb:* something caused to stay in your mind permanently (as in memory)		

Authors' Presentation of Ideas Anchor Chart

Name: _____

Date: _____

- How do authors introduce (or begin) their presentation of ideas?
  - With a story
  - With facts or statistics
  - With questions that get the reader thinking
  - With some background information on the topic or idea
- What types of evidence do authors use to inform or persuade the reader about a claim they are making?
  - Facts about a particular topic
  - Statistics to support an idea or claim
  - Statistics to inform
  - Quotes from experts
  - Stories to give meaning or examples
- How do authors use text features to inform or persuade the reader about a claim they are making?
  - Photographs to make the reader see
  - Photographs to make the reader feel
  - Sidebars to explain some important concept
  - Large fonts to make an idea or quote stand out

Learning from Frightful's Perspective

Chapter 15

Name: _____

Date: _____

Chapter 15: "A Pal Finds a Pal"	**Focus question:** Several characters in this chapter face challenges, including Frightful, Sam, and Mole. What challenges do characters in this chapter encounter, and how do they overcome them?	
Words I Found Difficult: **Glossary:** falconer—*noun:* a person who hunts with falcons or hawks and trains them for hunting incognito—*adverb:* keeping one's true identity secret (as by using a different name or disguise) thicket—*noun:* a group of bushes or small trees that grow close together pellet—*noun:* a wad of indigestible material (as of bones and fur) regurgitated by a bird of prey	**My thoughts:**	**Evidence from the text:**

EXPEDITIONARY
LEARNING

Affixes Resource

Prefixes and Suffixes

Name: _____

Date: _____

Prefixes	Meaning	Example	New Word
anti-	against	antifrost	
bio-, bi-	life	biology	
de-	opposite	defrost	
dis-	not, opposite of	disagree	
eco-	environment	ecofriendly	
en-, em-	cause of	encode, embrace	
fore-	before	forecast	
in-, im-	in	infield, inside	
in-, im-, il-, ir-	not	incorrect, impossible	
inter-	between	interact	
intro-	into, with, inward	introduce	
man-, manu-	hand, make, do	manicure, manual	
mid-	middle	midway	
mis-	wrongly	misfire	
non-	not	nonsense	
over-	beyond	overlook	
pre-	before	prefix	
pro-	for, forward	propel	
re-	again	return	

sem-, semi-	half	semicircle	
sub-	under	submarine	
super-	over or above	superstar	
trans-	across	transport	
un-	not	unfriendly	
under-	below	undersea	

Suffixes	Meaning	Example	New Word
-able, -ible	can be done	comfortable	
-al, -ial	having characteristics of	personal	
-cide, -cides	to kill	pesticide	
-ed	past-tense verbs	hopped	
-en	made of	wooden	
-er	comparative	higher	
-er, -or	one who	worker, actor	
-est	comparative	biggest	
-ful	full of	careful	
-ic	having characteristics of	electronic	
-ing	action or process	running	
-ion, -tion	act, process	promotion	
-ist	one that performs an action	cyclist	
-ity, -ty	state of	beauty	
-ive, -ative,	performs an action	active	
-less	without	fearless	
-ly	in a certain manner	quickly	
-ment	action or process	enjoyment	
-ness	state of, condition of	kindness	
-ology	study	zoology	
-ory	relating to, characterized by	memory	
-ous, -eous, -ious	possessing the qualities of	joyous	
-s, -es	more than one	books, boxes	

Research Vocabulary Graphic Organizer

Name: _____

Date: _____

Word from the Text	What do you think it means?	What strategy helped you determine the meaning? (CC = Context Clues A + R = Affixes + Root Words RM = Resource Material)	What is the dictionary's definition of this word?
1.			
2.			
3.			
4.			

Learning from Frightful's Perspective
Chapter 16

Name: _____

Date: _____

Chapter 16: "Frightful and Oksi Run the Show"	**Focus question:** Several moments in this chapter show strong relationships between the characters. What relationships are written about? How do we know they are strong relationships?	
Words I Found Difficult:		
Glossary: thermal—*noun:* a rising body of warm air hacking porch—*noun:* a board on which a hawk is fed	**My thoughts:**	**Evidence from the text:**

Learning from Frightful's Perspective

Chapter 17

Name: _____

Date: _____

Chapter 17: "Frightful Feels the Call of the Sky"	**Focus question:** When migration time was getting close, what changes started happening that told the birds it was time to go south or west?	
Words I Found Difficult:		
Glossary:		
nestling—*noun:* a young bird that has not left the nest	**My thoughts:**	**Evidence from the text:**
ravenously—*adverb:* very eagerly or greedily wanting food, satisfaction, or gratification		
paternalism—*adverb:* acting like a father		
cupola—*noun:* a small structure built on top of a roof		

Context Clues Resource

The first way to figure out the meaning of a new word is from its context. The *context* is the other words or sentences that are around the new word. Here are some strategies, or clues, for unlocking the meaning of a new word.

Clue 1: Search for a definition, a statement giving the meaning of a word.

Clue 2: Search for a synonym, a word or words that mean almost the same thing.

Clue 3: Search for an antonym, a word or words that mean the opposite of a word.

Clue 4: Reread the sentence and substitute a word that seems to make sense in the context.

If the word still does not make sense after using context clues, check a dictionary.

Using Context Clues Practice Sheet

Name: _____

Date: _____

Directions: Read the following statements. Use a context clue to find the meaning of the bold word in each statement.

Rachel Carson's work as a writer and scientist advocating for the needs of the environment captured people's attention. Her book, *Silent Spring*, began a new age of awareness about pollution and other threats in the natural world. Because Rachel Carson spoke out about the silence of birds and worked to protect the natural world, she became known as an **environmentalist**.

Search for a definition for **environmentalist** in the sentences around the word. What definition does the text provide?

_____

_____

_____

Rachel Carson wrote about an American town where all life used to live in harmony with its surroundings. She told people that **environment** changed when pesticides were used in that setting.

Search for a synonym for **environment** in the sentences around it. What synonym does the text provide?

_____

_____

_____

Chemical manufacturers were furious with Rachel Carson. They disagreed with her message as an environmentalist and called her a hysterical fanatic. They claimed that pesticides were perfectly **benign**, not harmful as Carson claimed, and there was no need to protect the natural world.

Search for an antonym for **benign**. What antonym does the text provide? What does **benign** mean?

_____

_____

_____

_____

_____

_____

_____

Comparing and Contrasting Authors' Presentation Graphic Organizer

Name: _____

Date: _____

Text 1 Title: "Biological Energy – Here, Let Me Fix It!"	Compare and Contrast the Authors' Presentation	Text 2 Title: "A New Home for DDT"
How does the author **introduce** the article?	How are they similar? How are they different?	How does the author **introduce** the article?
What **claim** does the author make?	How are they similar? How are they different?	What **claim** does the author make?
What type of **evidence** does the author include?	How are they similar? How are they different?	What type of **evidence** does the author include?
How does the author use **text features** (photographs, graphs, diagrams, etc.)?	How are they similar? How are they different?	How does the author use **text features** (photographs, graphs, diagrams, etc.)?

Which article is more effective in its argument? Why?

_____

_____

_____

_____

_____

_____

_____

_____

_____

_____

_____

_____

_____

_____

_____

_____

_____

_____

_____

_____

_____

_____

_____

_____

Learning from Frightful's Perspective

Chapter 18

Name: _____

Date: _____

Chapter 18: "The Earth Calls Frightful"	**Focus question:** What can you infer (or figure out based on evidence from the text) about the people on Hook Mountain? What traits would you used to describe these people?	
Words I Found Difficult:		
Glossary:		
Galapagos Islands— *noun:* the volcanic islands off the coast of Ecuador (to which they belong) in the eastern Pacific Ocean	**My thoughts:**	**Evidence from the text:**
winter solstice—*noun:* the time at which the sun appears at noon at its lowest altitude above the horizon; in the Northern Hemisphere it is usually around December 22		
magnetic pull—*noun:* the earth has two magnet-like pulls made by swirling motions of molten iron, one at the North Pole and one at the South Pole		

Digital Resources on DDT

Name: _____

Date: _____

Website URL	Description of Website
www.discoveriesinmedicine.com/Com-En/DDT.html#bDDT	This website is a general information website. It defines what DDT is, how it is used, its benefits, and its dangers.
www.panna.org/issues/persistent-poisons/the-ddt-story	This is the website for the Pesticide Action Network. It gives breakdowns on what foods and where in our bodies DDT can still be found. It also discusses why DDT is not the only solution for malaria.
www.nothingbutnets.net	This is the website of a nonprofit organization, Nothing But Nets, committed to helping end the malaria epidemic. This website informs about malaria, preventive measures against malaria, and the treatment of malaria in developing countries.
http://animals.nationalgeographic.com/animals/birds/peregrine-falcon/	This is a *National Geographic* website with general information about the peregrine falcon.
http://news.nationalgeographic.com/news/2006/08/060801-ddt-malaria.html	This is a *National Geographic* article about the use of DDT in the fight against malaria.

Exit Ticket

Using Digital Resources

Name: _____

Date: _____

On a scale from 1 to 5, how comfortable were you finding information from digital resources?

1	2	3	4	5
I feel lost		OK, but need some help		Totally confident

Were you able to find the information you need with the digital resources given, or do you need more sources?

☐　I'm OK with what we have

☐　I need more sources

What, if anything, was difficult about researching with digital resources?

_____

_____

_____

_____

_____

_____

_____

_____

_____

_____

_____

Learning from Frightful's Perspective

Chapter 19

Name: _____

Date: _____

Chapter 19: "Destiny Is on Wing"	**Focus question:** Where did Frightful decide to nest? Who was the tierce that would be her mate?	
Words I Found Difficult:		
Glossary:		
contentment—*noun:* the state of being happy and satisfied	**My thoughts:**	**Evidence from the text:**
accumulated—*verb:* gathered or acquired (something) gradually as time passes		
biological clock—*noun:* a system in the body that controls the occurrence of natural processes		
conservation—*noun:* the protection of animals, plants, and natural resources		

Mid-Unit Assessment

Comparing and Contrasting Two Texts: Simulated Research

Name: _____

Date: _____

Learning Targets

- I can compare how different authors portray the same idea or event. (RI.6.9)
- I can conduct short research projects to answer a question. (W.6.7)
- I can use several sources in my research. (W.6.7)
- I can refocus or refine my question when appropriate. (W.6.7)
- I can gather relevant information from a variety of sources. (W.6.8)
- I can assess the credibility of each source I use. (W.6.8)
- I can quote or paraphrase what others say about my topic while avoiding plagiarism. (W.6.8)
- I can provide a list of sources I used to gather information in a bibliography. (W.6.8)
- I can use a variety of strategies to determine the meaning of unknown words and phrases. (L.6.4)
- I can use context to determine the meaning of a word or phrase. (L.6.4.a)
- I can use common Greek and Latin affixes and roots as clues to help me determine the meaning of a word (e.g., *audience, auditory, audible*). (L.6.4.b)
- I can use resource materials (glossaries, dictionaries, thesauruses) to help me determine or clarify the pronunciation, meaning of key words and phrases, and parts of speech. (L.6.4.c)
- I can check the accuracy of my guess about the meaning of a word or phrase by using resource materials. (L.6.4.d)

Directions

- Today you will be reading two articles: "DDT Spray Scares Mosquitoes Away, Study Finds" and "You Think You Have It Tough?" Both are informational articles about mosquitoes, malaria, and DDT.
- After reading the first article, "DDT Spray Scares Mosquitoes Away, Study Finds," complete the Mid-Unit Assessment: Comparing and Contrasting Two Texts: Simulated Research Graphic Organizer identical to the ones you have been completing in your Researcher's Notebook.
- After reading the second article, "You Think You Have It Tough?" complete the Mid-Unit Assessment: Comparing and Contrasting Authors' Presentation Graphic Organizer identical to the one from previous lessons.

DDT Spray Scares Mosquitoes Away, Study Finds
(Assessment Text)

Reuters, UK Edition

Washington

Date: August 9, 2007

(Reuters)—Mosquitoes that carry malaria, dengue fever and yellow fever avoid homes that have been sprayed with DDT, researchers reported on Wednesday.

The chemical not only repels the disease-carrying insects physically, but its irritant and toxic properties helps keep them away, the researchers reported in the Public Library of Science journal PLoS ONE.

They estimate that DDT spray reduced the risk of disease **transmission** by nearly three-quarters.

Malaria affects more 40 percent of the world's population, killing more than a million people every year, most of them young children.

DDT use has been **discontinued** in most countries because of fears the pesticide may cause cancer and because of its potential effects on animals such as birds.

But the World Health Organization last year recommended the use of DDT in places like Africa where malaria is still common, saying the benefits outweighed the risks.

In the study, Dr. Donald Roberts of the Uniformed Services University of the Health Sciences in Bethesda, Maryland and colleagues tested DDT against *Aedes aegypti* mosquitoes in Thailand.

This species of mosquito does not carry malaria but it can transmit dengue and yellow fever.

"In huts sprayed with DDT, 59 of the 100 mosquitoes would not enter. Of the 41 that enter, 2 would die and fall to the floor," the researchers wrote.

Only 27 mosquitoes could theoretically bite and survive.

They said over a 24-hour period, DDT use would reduce the risk of a mosquito bite by 73 percent.

The researchers said the effects should hold for other species of mosquitoes, including Anopheles mosquitoes, which do transmit malaria.

"The historical record of malaria control operations show that DDT is the most cost-effective chemical for malaria control. Even now DDT is still considered to be the cheapest and most effective chemical for use in house spray operations," the researchers wrote.

Two other chemicals were also effective, the researchers found. "In huts sprayed with alphacypermethrin, all 100 mosquitoes would enter the house. Of the 100 that entered, 15 would die. Of the remaining 85, 46 would exit prematurely and 9 of those would die," they wrote.

This translated to 61 percent effectiveness.

"In huts sprayed with dieldrin, all 100 mosquitoes would enter the house," they wrote. Just eight mosquitoes that could take a blood meal and survive for a 92 percent protection, but it was likely the mosquitoes could develop resistance to this chemical, they said.

You Think You Have It Tough?

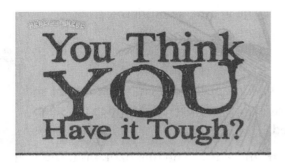

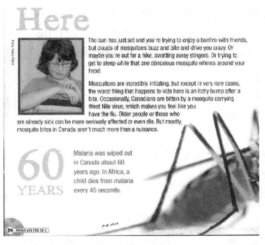

Reproduced with the permission of Canada's History Society.

Reproduced with the permission of Canada's History Society.

Poke. Slap. Itch.

What comes next is very different for you and for someone your age in other countries.

Here

The sun has just set and you're trying to enjoy a bonfire with friends, but clouds of mosquitos buzz and bite and drive you crazy. Or maybe you're out for a hike, swatting away stingers. Or trying to get sleep while that one obnoxious mosquito whines around your head.

Mosquitos are incredibly irritating, but except in very rare cases, the worst thing that happens to kids here is an itchy bump after a bite. Occasionally, Canadians are bitten by a mosquito carrying West Nile virus, which makes you feel like you have the flu. Older people or those who are already sick can be more seriously affected or even die. But mostly, mosquito bites in Canada aren't much more than a nuisance.

60 Years

Malaria was wiped out in Canada about 60 years ago. In Africa, a child dies from malaria every 45 seconds.

There

Some species of mosquito have a parasite—another tiny creature living off of them—that moves into humans' blood stream when that mosquito bites. The result is malaria, a disease that kills close to one million people every year, mostly children. An infected child who doesn't die may still be left paralyzed, brain damaged or blind.

Poorer people are more likely to live in conditions where mosquitoes breed. That means they are also more likely to get bitten and more likely to get malaria and other diseases. Malaria occurs in parts of the Caribbean, Asia, Africa, the Middle East and South America. It can be treated with drugs if it's discovered right away, but many people can't afford those treatments.

$10

There's an easy way to fight malaria and other diseases carried by mosquitoes: bed nets. These long-lasting nets keep bugs from biting kids in the night. One $10 donation buys a net that's been treated with insecticide. It can protect up to five children. The Canadian charity Spread the Net has sent more than half a million bed nets to the African countries where malaria problems are the worst.

Mid-Unit Assessment

Comparing and Contrasting Two Texts: Simulated Research Graphic Organizer

Name: _____

Date: _____

Source Information	Claims/Central Ideas *(Paraphrase the benefits or harmful consequences.)*	Details/Evidence
Source title:		
Author:		
Date:		
Source type *(newspaper article, book, website, video, etc.)*:		
Credible? Yes / No *(Use your Credibility Checklist to guide you.)*		

Does this source help you refocus or refine your research question in any way? How?

What new questions would you like answered before making your claim about DDT?

Mid-Unit Assessment

Comparing and Contrasting Authors' Presentation Graphic Organizer

Name: _____

Date: _____

Text 1 Title: "DDT Spray Scares Mosquitoes Away, Study Finds"	Compare and Contrast the Authors' Presentation	Text 2 Title: "You Think You Have It Tough?"
How does the author **introduce** the article?	How are they similar? How are they different?	How does the author **introduce** the article?
What **claim** does the author make?	How are they similar? How are they different?	What **claim** does the author make?
What type of **evidence** does the author include?	How are they similar? How are they different?	What type of **evidence** does the author include?
How does the author use **text features** (photographs, graphs, diagrams, etc.)?	How are they similar? How are they different?	How does the author use **text features** (photographs, graphs, diagrams, etc.)?

Which article is more effective in providing information or in building an argument? Why?

_____

_____

_____

_____

_____

_____

_____

_____

_____

_____

_____

_____

_____

_____

_____

_____

_____

_____

_____

_____

_____

_____

_____

Mid-Unit Assessment

Research Vocabulary Graphic Organizer

Using Multiple Strategies to Determine the Meaning of Words

Name: _____

Date: _____

- Each of these words comes from the article "DDT Spray Scares Mosquitoes Away, Study Finds."
- Refer to the article in order to use context clues to determine word meaning.
- Refer to your affixes list in order to use affixes + root words to determine word meaning.
- Refer to a resource material to confirm or revise your initial meaning.

Word from the Text	What do you think it means?	What strategy helped you determine the meaning? (CC = Context Clues A + R = Affixes + Root Words RM = Resource Material)	What is the dictionary's definition of this word?
1. transmission			
2. discontinued			
3. colleagues			

EXPEDITIONARY
LEARNING

Credibility Checklist

Name: _____

Date: _____

Title of article: _____

Source Information	Most Credible	Fairly Credible	Least Credible
Author	Expert in the field	Educated on the topic	Little or no information about the author
Date	Recently published or revised	Outdated	No date listed
Source Type	Official websites, institutional sites, academic journals, reputable news sources	Published material	Unfamiliar websites
Publisher	Publisher's relationship to the topic is balanced or neutral	Publisher is sponsored by a trusted source	Clearly biased or favoring a position for a purpose

Cascading Consequences Codes for Text References

Name: _____

Date: _____

Directions: Refer to the codes in parentheses to reference the article, video, graph, chart, table, diagram, or world map. Add this code to the cascading consequences chart to cite the source of the evidence.

Resources	Benefits of DDT Cascading Consequences Chart	Harmful Consequences of DDT Cascading Consequences Chart
Article	"The Exterminator" (EX)	"Welcome Back" (WB)
	"Double Whammy" (EX/D.W.)	"Rachel Carson: Sounding the Alarm on Pollution" (R.C. SA)
	"Public Fear" (EX/P.F.)	
	"Seriously Sick" (EX/S.S.)	
	"Killer Genes" (EX/K.G.)	
Video	"John Stossel – DDT" (V-J.S.)	"DDT – Dichloro-diphenyl-trichloroethane" (V-DDT)
Graphs and Charts	DDT Bad, Malaria much worse (world map)	Lake Kariba, Africa DDT Levels (diagram)
	Malaria Trends in South Africa (graph)	DDT in Human Body Fat in United States (table)
	Increases in Malaria for Countries in South America, 1993–1995 (graph)	DDT in Breast Milk (graph)
	DDT and Malaria in Ceylon (graph)	Changes in Thickness of Eggshells (graph)

Harmful Consequences of DDT Cascading Consequences Chart Example

Name: _____

Date: _____

Unit 1	Unit 2
"Welcome Back" (WB)	"Rachel Carson: Environmentalist and Writer" (R.C. E&W)
"Rachel Carson: Sounding the Alarm on Pollution" (R.C. SA)	Paul Müller (PM)
	"Biological Energy – Here, Let Me Fix It!" (BE)
	"How DDT Harmed Hawks and Eagles" (DDTH&E)

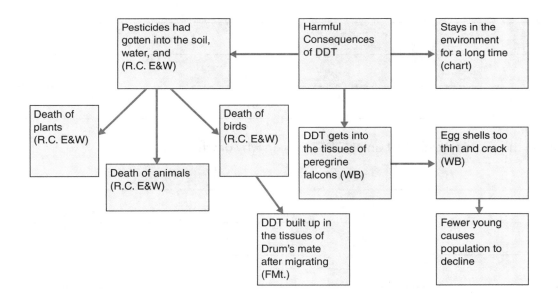

Exit Ticket

Reflecting on My Beliefs about DDT

Name: _____

Date: _____

1. What was a particularly *persuasive* piece of evidence you reflected on today? This evidence probably caused you to pause and think more deeply about what you were reading about and the impact it may have on our environment or people. Share your thoughts about this piece of evidence.

    _____

    _____

    _____

    _____

    _____

    _____

    _____

2. Should the world rethink the ban on DDT? Explain why or why not.

    _____

    _____

    _____

    _____

    _____

    _____

    _____

Entrance Ticket

Goldilocks's Rule for Choosing Books

Five-Finger Rule: Read the first two pages. Every time you come to a word that you don't know or can't define, put one finger up. If you get to five fingers before the end of the first page, STOP! This is probably not a good book to read on your own.

How many words did you not know on the first two pages? _____

_____

The Page 2 Check: Read the first two pages. At the end of the second page, stop and check for understanding. First try to summarize what you read so far. Does it make sense? If not, STOP!

Summarize:

_____

_____

_____

Did it make sense? _____

The Page 5 Check: Read the first five pages. At the end of the fifth page, stop and ask yourself: "Is this book making me think?" If you have not had to stop and think or clarify, STOP!

Are you thinking? _____

Did you have to clarify? _____

When you did clarify, how did you do it? _____

_____

So, is this a good book for you?

☐ No, because it's too hard.

☐ Yes, because it's just right.

☐ No, because it's too easy.

☐ No, because it's just right, but I'm not interested.

Reading Tracker and Reviewer's Notes Graphic Organizer

Name: _____

Date: _____

Book Title: _____

Directions: Complete one entry for each reading check-in.

Choices for Reviewer's Notes: Choose one idea to respond to for each entry.

- The most interesting/funniest/scariest scene was . . . because . . .

- A connection between this part of the book and what we are studying at school is . . . which helps me understand that . . .

- This part of the book reminds me of [other text, movie] because . . . which helps me understand that . . .

- A character I identify with/don't understand is . . . because . . .

- Something I learned about the world by reading this part of the book is . . . which seems important because . . .

Chapter Title(s) and Pages	Reading Tracker *(Briefly explain what happened in this part of the book.)*	Reviewer's Notes *(Respond to one of the ideas above.)*

Presenting a Claim and Findings Criteria Graphic Organizer

Name: _____

Date: _____

When preparing for and practicing your presentation, keep the following criteria in mind.

Presenter's Criteria	Partner Feedback *(Include one star and one wish.)*
I present my claim clearly.	
I present my findings in a logical order.	
I use descriptions, facts, and details to support my claim.	
I make eye contact with my audience.	
I use appropriate volume.	
I clearly pronounce my words.	
I include a visual display that clarifies information in my presentation.	
I use formal English. • Academic and domain-specific vocabulary • Language that expresses ideas precisely, eliminating wordiness and redundancy	

Who Are Stakeholders? Chart

Name: _____

Date: _____

stakeholder—*noun:* someone or something involved in or affected by a course of action

People	Living Things	Environment

Stakeholders' Impacts Chart

Name: _____

Date: _____

What happens when DDT is used?

Stakeholder				
How is the stakeholder affected by DDT?				
Is this positive (+) or negative (−)?				
If the consequence is negative, do you feel it is offset by a greater good elsewhere?				
How important is the stakeholder to you? (1 = very; 2 = somewhat; 3 = not much)				

Forming Evidence-Based Claims Graphic Organizer

Name: _____

Date: _____

Finding Details	Detail 1 (Reference)	Detail 2 (Reference)	Detail 3 (Reference)
I find interesting details that are related and that stand out to me from reading the text closely.			

Connecting the Details	What I think about detail 1:	What I think about detail 2:	What I think about detail 3:
I reread and think about the details and explain the connections I find among them.			
How I connect the details:			

Making a Claim	My claim about the text:
I state a conclusion that I have come to and can support with evidence from the text after reading and thinking about it closely.	

From Odell Education. Used by permission.

Checklist for Forming an Evidence-Based Claim

Claim

☐ The claim is a sentence that presents an issue.

☐ The claim is clear and specific.

☐ The claim gives the author's point of view or belief.

☐ The claim is something you can support with a solid argument.

☐ The claim uses domain-specific vocabulary.

Evidence

☐ The evidence is relevant.

☐ The evidence is factual and descriptive.

☐ The evidence is in a logical order.

☐ The evidence uses domain-specific vocabulary.

EXPEDITIONARY
LEARNING

Self- and Peer-Critique Graphic Organizer

Writer: _____

Critique Partner: _____

Date: _____

Claim	Yes or No	Comments
The claim presents an issue.		
The claim is expressed as the writer's belief or point of view.		
The first detail relates to the text or videos.		
The detail supports the claim.		
The second detail relates to the text or videos.		
The detail supports the claim.		
The third detail relates to the text or videos.		
The detail supports the claim.		
The claim is restated in a different way at the end.		

Video Critique Graphic Organizer

Tune in to Good Speaking

Name: _____

Date: _____

Criteria	Listener Feedback *(Include stars and steps.)*
The speaker made eye contact with the audience.	
The speaker used appropriate volume and pace.	
The speaker clearly pronounced and expressed words.	
The speaker included visual aids or displays that clarified information in the presentation.	
The speaker used formal English. • Academic and domain-specific vocabulary • Language that expressed ideas precisely, eliminating wordiness and redundancy	
The speaker presented the claim(s) clearly.	
The speaker presented information in a logical order or way that made sense and was easy to understand.	
The speaker used descriptions, facts, and details to support the claim.	

Task Card for Creating a Visual Aid

Creating the Cascading Consequences Chart Visual

1. Using a ruler, construct a draft line lightly in pencil for the title of the visual.

2. Write the title lightly in pencil using capital letters for the first word and last word and every important word in between.

3. Using a ruler, construct two draft lines lightly in pencil for the subtitles: Claim and Supporting Evidence.

4. Write the two subtitles lightly in pencil.

5. Using a ruler, construct draft lines lightly in pencil in the upper half of the paper for the claim.

6. Write the claim lightly in pencil.

7. Construct a circle around the claim using a compass or another larger object.

8. Using a ruler, construct draft lines lightly in pencil in the lower half of the paper for the three supporting pieces of evidence.

9. Neatly write the three supporting pieces of evidence lightly in pencil.

10. Use a ruler to construct three boxes around each piece of supporting evidence.

11. Go over the text, circle, and boxes with a black fine-tip marker.

12. Neatly erase all pencil marks.

13. Consider choosing four different colored pencils to shade the background of the text.

Creating the Stakeholders' Impacts Chart Visual

1. Using a ruler, construct a draft line lightly in pencil for the title of the visual.

2. Write the title lightly in pencil using capital letters for the first word and last word and every important word in between.

3. Using a ruler and pencil, construct the stakeholders chart that best highlights your claim. Include the text headings as part of the visual.

4. Using a ruler, construct draft lines for text. Neatly copy the text from the stakeholders draft.

5. Outline all pencil marks with a black fine-tip marker.

6. Neatly erase all pencil marks.

7. Consider choosing different colored pencils to shade the background of the text.

A Visual to Support My Claim

Name: _____

Date: _____

Claim:

Supporting
Evidence:

1	2	3

A Visual to Support My Claim

Name: _____

Date: _____

What happens when DDT is used?

Stakeholder					
How is the stakeholder affected by DDT?					
Is this positive (+) or negative(-)?					
If the consequence is negative, do you feel it is offset by greater good elsewhere?					
How important is the stakeholder to you?	1 = very; 2 = somewhat; 3 = not much				

Criteria for the Cascading Consequences Chart Visual

Name: _____

Date: _____

		Yes	Not Yet
Content	The claim is a sentence that states the issue and presents my belief or point of view.		
	Three pieces of evidence provide descriptions, facts, and details that support my claim.		
	Academic and domain-specific vocabulary are used.		
Visual Appeal	Text is free of spelling errors.		
	Text is free of mechanical and grammar errors.		
	Color adds to the interest.		
	Draft lines were used to guide text writing.		
	A ruler was used to construct three boxes for supporting evidence.		
	A compass was used to construct a circle for the claim.		
	All draft lines were neatly erased.		

Criteria for Stakeholders' Impacts Chart Visual

Name: _____

Date: _____

		Yes	Not Yet
Content	Four stakeholders are identified.		
	An explanation defines how each stakeholder is affected by the position or option chosen.		
	The effect for each stakeholder is indicated as intentional or a side effect.		
	Academic and domain-specific vocabulary is used (10 words).		
Visual Appeal	Text is free of spelling errors		
	Text is free of mechanical and grammar errors.		
	Color adds to the interest.		
	Draft lines were used to guide text writing.		
	A ruler was used to construct three boxes for supporting evidence.		
	All draft lines were neatly erased.		

Presenting a Claim and Findings Criteria Peer-Critique Form

Speaker's Name: _____

Listener's Name: _____

Speaker's Criteria	Partner Feedback *(Include one star and one wish.)*
The claim was clearly presented, stating the issue and the speaker's point of view.	
Findings were presented in a logical order.	
Descriptions, facts, and details supported the claim.	
Eye contact was made with the audience.	
Appropriate volume made it easy to hear.	
Words were pronounced clearly.	
A visual display was used and clarified information in the presentation.	
Formal English enhanced the presentation. • Academic and domain-specific vocabulary (at least 10) • Language that expressed ideas precisely, eliminating wordiness and redundancy	

Exit Ticket

Preparing for My Presentation

Name: _____

Date: _____

1. What do I need to do to prepare for the End-of-Unit 2 Assessment on my:

   a. Visual aid?

   _____

   _____

   b. Notecards?

   _____

   _____

   c. Speaking techniques?

   _____

   _____

2. What are my priorities in order to be prepared?

   _____

   _____

3. What do I feel most confident about?

   _____

   _____

Presenting a Claim and Findings Criteria

Name: _____

Date: _____

When preparing for and practicing your presentation, keep the following criteria in mind.

Presenter's Criteria	Partner Feedback *(Include one star and one wish.)*
I present my claim clearly.	
I present my findings in a logical order.	
I use descriptions, facts, and details to support my claim.	
I make eye contact with my audience.	
I use appropriate volume.	
I clearly pronounce my words.	
I include a visual display that clarifies information in my presentation.	
I use formal English. • Academic and domain-specific vocabulary • Language that expresses ideas precisely, eliminating wordiness and redundancy	

Gallery Walk Presentation Checklist

Name: _____

Date: _____

Speaker's Name	Had a claim and three pieces of evidence.	Made eye contact and used clear pronunciation.	Had a clarifying visual and used it.	Share a star!

End-of-Unit 2 Assessment

Presenting a Claim and Findings

Name: _____

Date: _____

Learning Targets

- I can present claims and findings in a logical order. (SL.6.4)

- I can support my main points with descriptions, facts, and details. (SL.6.4)

- I can use effective speaking techniques (appropriate eye contact, adequate volume, and clear pronunciation). (SL.6.4)

- I can include multimedia components and visual displays in a presentation to clarify information. (SL.6.5)

- I can adapt my speech for a variety of contexts and tasks, using formal English when indicated or appropriate. (SL.6.6)

Criteria	✓
I presented my claim clearly.	
I presented my findings in a logical order.	
I used descriptions, facts, and details to support my claim.	
I made eye contact with my audience.	
I used appropriate volume.	
I clearly pronounced my words.	
I included a visual display that clarifies information in my presentation.	
I used formal English. • Academic and domain-specific vocabulary • Language that expressed ideas precisely, eliminating wordiness and redundancy	

Reading Tracker and Reviewer's Notes Graphic Organizer

Name: _____

Date: _____

Book Title: _____

Directions: Complete one entry for each reading check-in.

Choices for Reviewer's Notes: Choose one idea to respond to for each entry.

- The most interesting/funniest/scariest scene was . . . because . . .
- A connection between this part of the book and what we are studying at school is . . . which helps me understand that . . .
- This part of the book reminds me of [other text, movie] because . . . which helps me understand that . . .
- A character I identify with/don't understand is . . . because . . .
- Something I learned about the world by reading this part of the book is . . . which seems important because . . .

Chapter Title(s) and Pages	Reading Tracker *(Briefly explain what happened in this part of the book.)*	Reviewer's Notes *(Respond to one of the ideas above.)*

Model Position Paper

"Hydraulic Fracturing"

Question: Should New York State use hydraulic fracturing to collect natural gas?

Hydraulic fracturing, or "fracking," is a drilling process used to collect natural gas. Like oil and coal, natural gas is an important source of energy in the world. However, finding a good way to extract it from the earth has been a challenge. Based on research, my position is that hydraulic fracturing is a process that should be used to collect natural gas, but only if it is done safely and with enforced regulations. Hydraulic fracturing has significant benefits to both the environment and to people. However, there are dangers in using it too much or going too fast.

One important reason that hydraulic fracturing should be used is that it is better for the environment than other forms of energy we use. In the article "Good Gas, Bad Gas" in *National Geographic,* it says, "Natural gas burns much cleaner than coal. In part because American power plants have been switching from coal to cheap gas, U.S. emissions of CO_2 from fossil fuels fell last year, even as the world set another record." This means that by switching from coal to natural gas collected by hydraulic fracturing, we can make the air cleaner and do less damage to the ozone layer.

Another strong reason that hydraulic fracturing should be used is that it can really help people. According to *Business Insider,* "With the advances in drilling and hydraulic fracturing, the U.S. shale boom could add as much as $690 billion a year to the GDP and create up to 1.7 million jobs." This is important because there are people in New York who would apply for these jobs, and this could help them support their families.

However, there are some risks, and hydraulic fracturing needs to be done safely and with clear regulations. This is important because hydraulic fracturing could do great harm to our water supply. The article "Fracking Fuels Energy Debate" in *Science News for Kids* states, "scientists found that the water from wells within 1 kilometer of fracking sites had much higher levels of dissolved methane than water from wells farther away." This quote clearly shows that fracking, or hydraulic fracturing, has the potential to do environmental damage, and maybe even damage the people who drink the water.

This is a very complicated issue to decide, and could have many benefits as well as harmful consequences. However, if hydraulic fracturing is done safely and is regulated, the benefits for the environment and for people would make it worth it.

Sources:

http://ngm.nationalgeographic.com/2012/12/methane/lavelle-text

www.businessinsider.com/5-ways-to-make-5m-new-jobs-by-2020-2013-7

https://student.societyforscience.org/article/fracking-fuels-energy-debate

Author's Presentation of Events Graphic Organizer

Name: _____

Date: _____

How does the author introduce (or begin) his or her presentation of events?

☐   With a story

☐   With facts or statistics

☐   With questions that get the reader thinking

☐   With some background information on the topic or event

What is the author's claim, or position?

_____

_____

What are the reasons the author chose this position?

•   _____

•   _____

•   _____

•   _____

How could the author's claim and reasons be written as an argument?

_____

_____

_____

_____

What transitional words or phrases does the author use to move from one reason to another?

•   _____

•   _____

•   _____

What types of evidence does the author use to inform or persuade the reader?

☐ Facts about a particular topic

☐ Statistics to support an idea or claim

☐ Statistics to inform

☐ Quotes from experts

☐ Stories to give meaning or examples

Which text features does the author use to inform or persuade the reader?

☐ Photographs to make the reader see

☐ Photographs to make the reader feel

☐ Sidebars to explain some important concept

☐ Large fonts to make an idea or quote stand out

Position Paper Argument Rubric

Criteria	CCSS	4 Essays at This Level:	3 Essays at This Level:	2 Essays at This Level:	1 Essays at This Level:	0 Essays at This Level:
CLAIM AND REASONS: the extent to which the essay conveys complex ideas and information clearly and accurately in order to logically support the author's argument.	W.2 R.1–9	• Clearly introduce the text and the claim in a manner that is compelling and follows logically from the task and purpose. • Claim and reasons demonstrate insightful analysis of the text(s). • Acknowledges counterclaim(s) skillfully and smoothly.	• Clearly introduce the text and the claim in a manner that follows from the task and purpose. • Claim and reasons demonstrate grade-appropriate analysis of the text(s). • Acknowledges counterclaim(s) appropriately and clearly.	• Introduce the text and the claim in a manner that follows generally from the task and purpose. • Claim and reasons demonstrate a literal comprehension of the text(s). • Acknowledges counterclaim(s) awkwardly.	• Introduce the text and the claim in a manner that does not logically follow from the task and purpose. • Claim and reasons demonstrate little under-standing of the text(s). • Does not acknowledge counterclaim(s).	• Claim and reasons demonstrate a lack of comprehension of the text(s) or task.
COMMAND OF EVIDENCE: the extent to which the essay presents evidence from the provided	W.9 R.1–9	• Develop the argument with relevant, well-chosen facts, definitions, concrete details, quotations, or	• Develop the argument with relevant facts, definitions, details, quotations, or other information	• Partially develop the argument of the essay with the use of some textual evidence, some of which may be irrelevant.	• Demonstrate an attempt to use evidence, but only develop ideas with minimal, occasional	• Provide no evidence or provide evidence that is completely irrelevant.

Criterion	Standards					
texts to support the argument.		• other information and examples from the text(s). • Sustain the use of varied, relevant evidence. • Skillfully and logically explain how evidence supports ideas.	• and examples from the text(s). • Sustain the use of relevant evidence, with some lack of variety. • Logically explain how evidence supports ideas.	• Use relevant evidence inconsistently. • Sometimes logically explain how evidence supports ideas.	• evidence that is generally invalid or irrelevant. • Attempt to explain how evidence supports ideas.	• Does not explain how evidence supports ideas.
COHERENCE, ORGANIZATION, AND STYLE: the extent to which the essay logically organizes complex ideas, concepts, and information using formal style and precise language.	W.2 L.3 L.6	• Exhibit clear organization, with the skillful use of appropriate and varied transitions to create a unified whole and enhance meaning. • Establish and maintain a formal style, using grade-appropriate, stylistically sophisticated language and domain-specific vocabulary with a notable sense of voice.	• Exhibit clear organization, with the use of appropriate transitions to create a unified whole. • Establish and maintain a formal style using precise language and domain-specific vocabulary. • Provide a concluding statement or section that follows from the claim and reasons presented.	• Exhibit some attempt at organization, with inconsistent use of transitions. • Establish but fail to maintain a formal style, with inconsistent use of language and domain-specific vocabulary. • Provide a concluding statement or section that follows generally the claim and reasons presented.	• Exhibit little attempt at organization, or attempts to organize are irrelevant to the task. • Lack a formal style, using language that is imprecise or inappropriate for the text(s) and task. • Provide a concluding statement or section that is illogical or unrelated	• Exhibit no evidence of organization. • Use language that is predominantly incoherent or copied directly from the text(s). • Do not provide a concluding statement or section.

CONTROL OF CONVENTIONS: the extent to which the essay demonstrates command of the conventions of standard English grammar, usage, capitalization, punctuation, and spelling. W.2 L.1 L.2	• Provide a concluding statement or section that is compelling and follows clearly from the claim and reasons presented. • Demonstrate grade-appropriate command of conventions, with few errors.	• Demonstrate grade-appropriate command of conventions, with occasional errors that do not hinder comprehension.	• Demonstrate emerging command of conventions, with some errors that may hinder comprehension.	to the claim and reasons presented. • Demonstrate a lack of command of conventions, with frequent errors that hinder comprehension.	• Are minimal, making assessment of conventions unreliable.

Exit Ticket

What do you think you will find most challenging in writing a paper like this?

_____

_____

_____

_____

_____

_____

_____

_____

_____

_____

_____

_____

_____

_____

_____

_____

_____

_____

EXPEDITIONARY
LEARNING

Steps to Writing a Position Paper

(Blank)

Name: _____

Date: _____

Prewrite

_____

_____

_____

_____

_____

Plan

_____

_____

_____

_____

_____

_____

Draft

_____

_____

_____

_____

_____

_____

_____

Revise

_____

_____

_____

_____

_____

Edit and Proofread

_____

_____

_____

_____

_____

Share

_____

_____

_____

_____

_____

Steps to Writing a Position Paper

(Tasks for Each Step)

Name: _____

Date: _____

Prewrite

Think before writing.

Understand your purpose, audience, and format.

Study the issue using available resources.

Record evidence from credible sources.

Plan

Organize your ideas before writing.

Create a prewriting plan.

Support your claims with clear reasons and relevant evidence.

Draft

Write your ideas in sentences and paragraphs.

Follow your prewriting plan.

Write the first draft of your paper.

Revise

Improve your ideas.

Add a hook, transition words, and domain-specific vocabulary.

Change the order of your reasons and evidence.

Add, change, clarify, and delete evidence.

Edit and Proofread

Focus on editing and proofreading.

Check for errors in grammar, spelling, and capitalization.

Share

Present your work.

Show your work to an audience.

Planning My Argument Graphic Organizer

Name: _____

Date: _____

Directions: Read and reflect on your Forming Evidence-Based Claims Graphic Organizer, your four notecards from the Gallery Walk, and the End-of-Unit 3 Assessment: Presenting a Claim and Findings teacher feedback.

What is a star in writing your claim and supporting evidence?

_____

_____

What is a next step in writing your claim and supporting evidence?

_____

_____

_____

Claim:

Reason:

_____

Supporting Evidence:

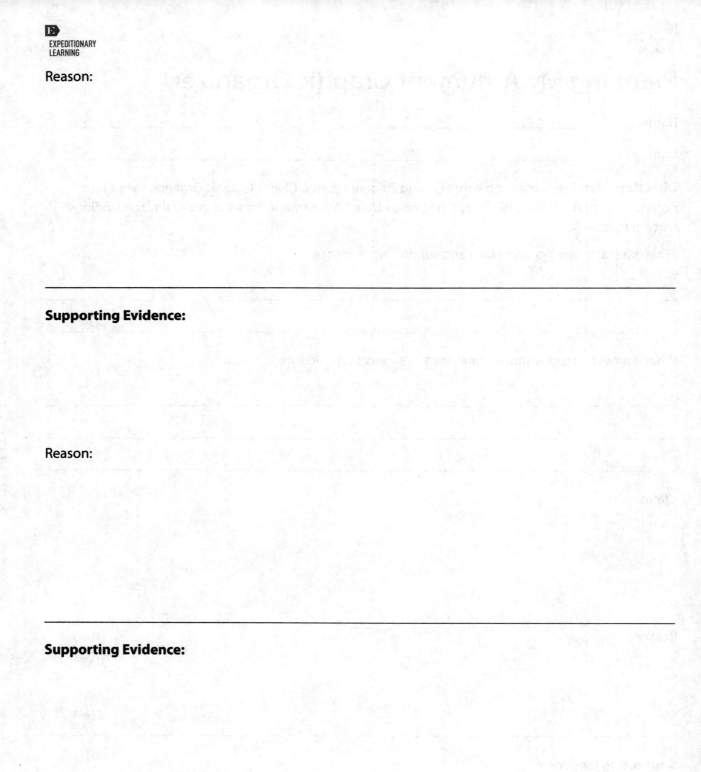

Reason:

Supporting Evidence:

Reason:

Supporting Evidence:

Checklist for Forming an Evidence-Based Claim

Claim

1. The claim is a sentence that presents an issue.
2. The claim is clear and specific.
3. The claim gives the author's point of view, or belief.
4. The claim is something on which you can build a solid argument.
5. The claim uses domain-specific vocabulary.

Evidence

1. The evidence is relevant.
2. The evidence is factual and descriptive.
3. The evidence is in a logical order.
4. The evidence uses domain-specific vocabulary.

Planning My Body Paragraphs Graphic Organizer

Name: _____

Date: _____

Body Paragraph 1

Transition:

First reason to support your claim. (Use your own words.)

Evidence to support your reason. (Cite evidence from your research materials.)

Connect evidence to your claim. (Use your own words.)

Body Paragraph 2

Transition:

First reason to support your claim. (Use your own words.)

Evidence to support your reason. (Cite evidence from your research materials.)

Connect evidence to your claim. (Use your own words.)

Body Paragraph 3

Transition:

First reason to support your claim. (Use your own words.)

Evidence to support your reason. (Cite evidence from your research materials.)

Connect evidence to your claim. (Use your own words.)

Domain-Specific Vocabulary and Transitions Graphic Organizer

Name: _____

Date: _____

Domain-Specific Vocabulary	Transitions

Parts of a Position Paper Anchor Chart

Name: _____

Date: _____

Introductory Paragraph

- Engages the reader: Introduces the topic with a strong opening statement; a hook or attention-grabber
- Connector: Links the reader from your opening statement to your claim
- States the claim: Gives your point of view
- Refers to three supporting reasons: Lets the reader know what you will present by using key words from the claim, but not the whole reasons

Body Paragraph 1

- Transition to reason: Begins the paragraph, puts information in a logical order
- Evidence: Facts, statistics, quotes, stories
- Link: Explains how your evidence supports your claim

Body Paragraph 2

- Transition to reason: Begins the paragraph, puts information in a logical order
- Evidence: Facts, statistics, quotes, stories
- Link: Explains how your evidence supports your claim

Body Paragraph 3

- Transition to reason: Begins the paragraph, puts information in a logical order
- Evidence: Facts, statistics, quotes, stories
- Link: Explains how your evidence supports your claim

Conclusion

- Restates the claim: Repeats your point of view in a different way
- Synthesizes: Combines the three reasons

- Analysis of topic and logical conclusion: Points out the relationship
- Clincher: A final, decisive argument or remark that answers, "So what is the point of raising this issue?"

Formal English

- Not casual language
- Language appropriate for official or important writing and speaking

Vocabulary

- Domain-specific
- Transition words and phrases

Writing Conventions

- Usage
- Grammar
- Mechanics

Mid-Unit Assessment

Position Paper Prompt

Learning Targets

- I can write arguments to support claims with clear reasons and relevant evidence. (W.6.1)
- I can create an introduction that states my main argument and foreshadows the organization of my piece. (W.6.1.a)
- I can construct a concluding statement or section that reinforces my main argument. (W.6.1.e)

Directions

- Write a position paper in which you respond to the following questions.
- Support your claim with relevant evidence from your research.
- Conclude your paper in a way that follows logically from your claim and evidence.

Prompt

- Do you believe DDT should be used despite its potentially harmful consequences in the natural world?
- Do the benefits of DDT outweigh its harmful consequences?

EXPEDITIONARY
LEARNING

Writing Reflections Graphic Organizer

Name: _____

Date: _____

Directions: Read your position paper with these reflection questions in mind.

What did I do well?

_____

_____

_____

_____

_____

What challenges did I have?

_____

_____

_____

_____

_____

What help do I need to make it better?

_____

_____

_____

_____

_____

Resource Reference Sheet

Transitions—Words That Connect Ideas

First	Second
One piece of evidence that points to this is	Another good example is
To begin	Secondly
Initially	Furthermore
One good example is	Another way to look at this is through
One reason is	Another example
One way this is true	Another example that helps support this is
It is important to note that	Another indication of this is
One way to look at this is through	Still
One notable example is	Even so
One reason this is important	In the same way
A great example is	Next
One example that stands out is	On the other hand
The best place to start is with	Even more compelling is
This can first be seen when	Another example that stands out is
For example	Similarly
For instance	Likewise
This can be clearly seen first of all when	Along with that, there is
	Moreover
	In addition
	Also
	In the same light
	Even more interesting is
	An even better example of this is
	An additional fact is
	Another strong indication was when

Third or Final	Conclusion
Lastly	So, it is clear to see that
A final great example	Accordingly
The final piece of evidence is	In summary
The last example that suggests this is	Consequently
Yet the best reason is	Thus
The final indication of this is	As a result
Most compelling is	In short
Even so	Therefore
The best and final reason is	When looking at the facts, it is evident that
The most important reason is	The evidence clearly points
On top of all that	All of this together means
The final example to note	With all of this
The last example that stands out is	The three examples, . . ., prove that
Most importantly	And so therefore
Accordingly	For all of these reasons, one can see that
Moreover	With all of this in mind
Adding to those	Due to all of these reasons
In addition to those	Together
Of course	One can see that
But most conclusive is	The evidence is clear
In the same light	And so it is
An even better example of this is	Truly

Slang, Casual, and Formal Messages

Text, Email, or Letter?

whuz up, bud

☐ Text

☐ Email

☐ Letter

Hey, buddy! Just checking to see what you're up to.

☐ Text

☐ Email

☐ Letter

Dear Son,

You have been in my thoughts. I'm wondering what activities you are involved with. Please write or call.

☐ Text

☐ Email

☐ Letter

Revision Checklist

Author: _____

Peer Editor: _____

Date: _____

Title: _____

_____

	Author		Editor	
	Star	**Step**	<u>**Star**</u>	**Step**
Claim and Reasons	_____	_____	_____	_____
Introduces topic	_____	_____	_____	_____
States claim	_____	_____	_____	_____
Supporting reasons	_____	_____	_____	_____
	_____	_____	_____	_____
Command of Evidence	_____	_____	_____	_____
Develops argument with evidence	_____	_____	_____	_____
Varied evidence (different kinds)	_____	_____	_____	_____
Evidence supports reasons	_____	_____	_____	_____
	_____	_____	_____	_____
Coherence, Organization, and Style	_____	_____	_____	_____
Includes transitions	_____	_____	_____	_____
In a logical order	_____	_____	_____	_____
Uses formal language	_____	_____	_____	_____
Uses domain-specific language	_____	_____	_____	_____
	_____	_____	_____	_____

Control of Conventions				
Spelling	_____	_____	_____	_____
Capitalization	_____	_____	_____	_____
Complete sentences	_____	_____	_____	_____
Correct word choice (usage)	_____	_____	_____	_____
	_____	_____	_____	_____

Formal or Informal—Can You Guess?

Name: _____

Date: _____

Passage 1

In the 1940s, the chemical industry developed pesticides that killed harmful insects and saved farmers and gardeners time and money. Over time, however, some of these chemicals hurt not only insects but also birds, mammals, and fish. Some scientists wrote about the dangers of pesticides, but few people paid attention.

By 1960, tens of thousands of fish, birds, and mammals had died. It was then that Rachel Carson, a marine biologist who was interested in nature, wrote *Silent Spring*. She did not oppose the use of all pesticides. But she wrote, "We have allowed these chemicals to be used with little or no advance investigation of their effect on the soil, water, wildlife, and man himself."

Passage 2

In the 1940s, some businesses made chemicals that helped farmers and gardeners. After a while, some of these chemicals hurt not only insects, but some other animals too. Some scientists wrote about the dangers of the chemicals, but not a lot of people paid attention.

By 1960, lots of animals died. Then a scientist named Rachel Carson, who was a nature nut, wrote *Silent Spring*. She wasn't totally against using all the chemicals. But she was pretty bent out of shape about them and thought people should check it out more before using them.

Which passage was formal?   Passage 1 _____   Passage 2 _____

Reasons why:

_____

_____

_____

_____

_____

_____

_____

Entrance Ticket

Plot Development

Plot: A series of events in the story that serve to move the story from its beginning through its climax, or turning point, and to a resolution of its conflicts. Plot is why the story happens and why the main character learns or grows, or begins or chooses something.

Explain the plot development of your novel thus far. Choose three to five events in the story that move the story toward the climax.

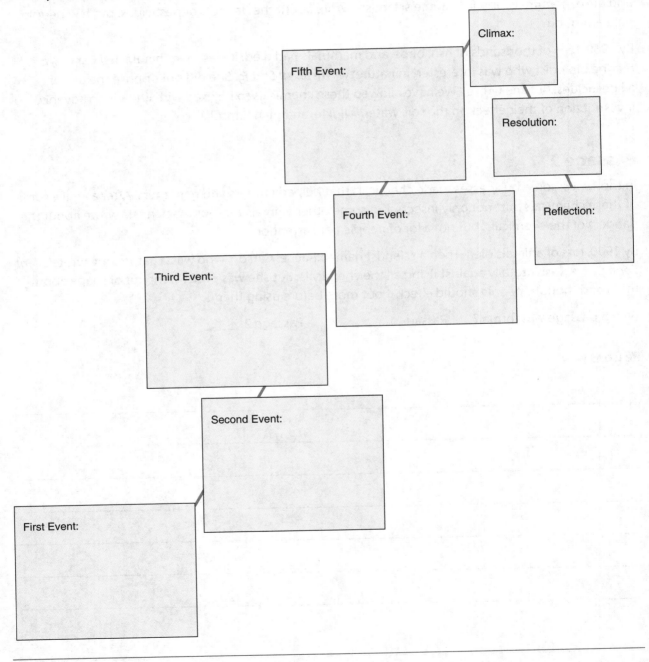

Position Paper Vocabulary Criteria

1. Grade-appropriate vocabulary
2. Stylistically sophisticated language (intellectually appealing)
3. Domain-specific (10+ vocabulary words)
4. Vocabulary with a notable sense of voice (words take a stand and speak for themselves)

Vocabulary Feedback

Name: _____

Partner's Name: _____

Date: _____

1. Grade-appropriate vocabulary

Star:

_____

Next step:

_____

2. Stylistically sophisticated language (intellectually appealing)

Star:

_____

Next step:

_____

3. Domain-specific (10+ vocabulary words)

Star:

_____

Next step:

_____

4. Vocabulary with a notable sense of voice (words take a stand and speak for themselves)

Star:

_____

Next step:

_____

End-of-Unit 3 Assessment

Position Paper Prompt

Learning Targets

- With support from peers and adults, I can use a writing process to produce clear and coherent writing. (W.6.5)
- I can identify when standard English is and isn't used. (L.6.1.e)
- I can convert language into standard English. (L.6.1.e)
- I can accurately use sixth-grade academic vocabulary to express my ideas. (L.6.6)
- I can use resources to build my vocabulary. (L.6.6)

Directions

- Using the feedback you have received from both your teacher and peers, as well as the lesson you received on the use of standard English in writing, revise your position paper to create a final published version.
- This should also include intentional use of the vocabulary you have acquired throughout the course of your research and study of DDT, its benefits, and its harmful consequences in the natural world.

Prompt

- Do you believe DDT should be used despite its potentially harmful consequences in the natural world?
- Do the benefits of DDT outweigh its harmful consequences?

Writing Process Reflection

Name: _____

Date: _____

Directions: Read the six steps of the writing process. Identify the steps that are stars and the steps that are next steps. Write star or next step with a reason on the line provided.

1. **Prewrite** (understand the purpose, study the issue, record evidence from credible sources)

    _____

    _____

    _____

    _____

2. **Plan** (organize ideas, create a prewriting plan, support claim with clear reasons and evidence)

    _____

    _____

    _____

    _____

3. **Draft** (write ideas in sentences/paragraphs, write first draft)

    _____

    _____

    _____

    _____

4. **Revise** (improve ideas, add hook, transitions, domain-specific vocabulary, change order of reasons and evidence, clarify or delete evidence)

    _____

    _____

    _____

    _____

5. **Edit and Proofread** (check for errors in grammar, spelling, punctuation, and capitalization)

_____

_____

_____

_____

6. **Share** (present your work, show your work to an audience)

_____

_____

_____

_____

Other Thoughts

7. How has following the steps in the writing process helped you improve your writing?

_____

_____

_____

_____

8. Share an important next step that you want to take as a writer. Explain how you will accomplish this.

_____

_____

_____

_____

Scientific Poster Model

Do the Benefits of DDT Outweigh Its Harmful Consequences?

Claim is stated.

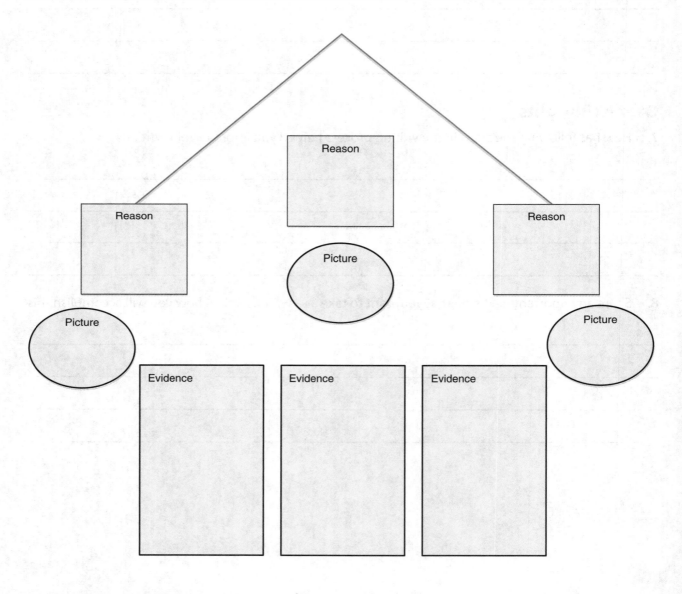

Scientific Poster Criteria Checklist

Guiding question as basis for title

☐ "Do the benefits of DDT outweigh its harmful consequences?"

Introduction

☐ Claim or position

Three reasons

☐ Arranged below the claim

☐ Placed in the same order as the body paragraphs

☐ Arrows or lines to connect reasons to claim

☐ Words or phrases, not complete sentences

Evidence: Facts, statistics, quotes, story

☐ Aligned with each reason it supports

☐ Linked or connected with lines or arrows

☐ Facts and statistics not in complete sentences

☐ Quotes—use quotation marks at the beginning and end of quotes

☐ Story—summarized in complete sentences

Conclusion

☐ Claim restated in a different way

☐ Complete sentences

☐ Could be expressed as a clincher

Possible text features to use as visuals

☐ Photographs

☐ Graphs, charts, tables

☐ Drawings

☐ Part of your cascading consequences chart

☐ Part of your stakeholders chart

☐ Sidebar

☐ Large font

☐ Captions